The Selfish Divorce

*How to Get the Most Important
Things from Your Breakup*

Greg W. Anderson

TABLE OF CONTENTS

When my ex announced she was going to get remarried, I decided to post something about it on Facebook. No, this isn't a story of a poorly considered FB post gone sour.

You can read the entire post in the following pages, but in essence what I said was:

I am so happy for her. She's an amazing woman. I wish them both the very best for the future.

The comments, both online and offline, came pouring in. Some thought it was a joke. Some thought I was being sarcastic. Many simply couldn't believe that you could "love" your ex.

I was interested in the response but I was also saddened. It is clear that so many people see their divorces as disasters and their exes as the devil. It doesn't have to be that way.

My own divorce allowed both my ex, Sarah, and me to face the future unburdened by anger, resentment, bitterness, and even huge attorney fees. Our approach allowed us to move into the future with the possibility of being the best versions of ourselves. This experience prompted me to write this book about the "selfish" divorce. As you'll read, the selfish divorce isn't what you think. It could easily be called the "selfless" divorce, because in the end, being selfless is adaptive and will lead to the best outcomes possible for you, your ex, and your children.

That said, here's what to expect from The Selfish Divorce:

In the first five chapters of this book, I'll tell you my life story, especially as it relates to relationships and marriage. At the end of each of these chapters, you'll see a section called "In the Rearview Mirror: Life Lessons from My Journey." Some of these lessons have to do with relationships and some don't. But they're all things I've learned in the School of Hard Knocks—and if possible, I'd like to help prevent you from taking any of the "classes" I did.

Chapters Six through Nine of this book are more tactical advice-oriented. In them, I explain exactly what I mean by "selfish divorce" and make a case for why you should consider taking this route if your own marriage is ending. I also share advice to help you....

Greg Anderson

Fall 2014

CHAPTER ONE

The Family Struggles

As its title suggests, the book you're reading is about divorce. In the following chapters I'll tell you about my experience with divorce, and I'll share the lessons I've learned. But first, so that you'll have a background understanding of my journey, there are some things I'd like to tell you about my childhood. Many of the lessons and worldviews I internalized as a kid had a direct impact on how I approached my relationships as an adult, and the same is probably true for you, too. So here goes!

Low Funds and High Tensions

I loved my dad and I was sorry to see him struggle for so much of his life. He was a good man who probably never realized his potential. But he never said anything negative. He worked hard in trying to provide for his family, and for most of my young life he worked at Geneva Steel.

During World War II the government opened a new steel plant in Vineyard, Utah, which is where I grew up (albeit decades after the 1940s). The plant was located there because it needed to be far from the west coast and safe in the event of an attack by the Japanese. After the war the plant eventually became Geneva Steel. Utah was an unlikely place for a steel plant as it was a long way removed from suppliers of the resources it needed and the end users of its products. These factors, along with environmental concerns and the decline in U.S. manufacturing, led to the plant's filing for bankruptcy and fading in and out of operation in the 1980s and 1990s.

The plant was a major employer in the area, and when the work slowed down, it had a significant impact on the local economy. One of those affected was my dad. He was laid off, and that had a serious effect on my life. Finances became very tight, and the conflict between my parents increased. As money ran low, the tension ran high.

It was clear that there were serious issues, but my parents didn't really argue in front of us five kids. I had three older brothers (I would later discover that the two oldest were from my mom's first marriage) and a younger sister. Instead of airing their arguments in front of us, my parents would leave my older brothers in charge, jump in our minivan, and just take off. At the time I wasn't sure where they were going but I intuitively sensed that they weren't going on a pleasant drive in the country. Often, I lay down on the couch and prayed for their safe return. I was born into a Mormon culture, and prayer was part of our home life. I was scared, but you wouldn't have known it from looking at me. I had learned to block out my emotions and act like everything was cool. And that had begun a year or so earlier, when I started first grade.

The "Art" of Concealment

When I entered elementary school, I wasn't as good as the other kids at reading. If you can't read in school, then you're going to fall behind in just about every subject as reading and writing are the main vehicles for learning in the public school system. So I wasn't just failing in reading and writing; I was failing in just about everything. I was sent to the resource room for my education, along with the other mentally and physically challenged kids. I was humiliated and ashamed but I never let anyone see that. Instead, I developed a cheerful and social persona. I decided that if I was dumb, I would at least be liked. And if I was cheerful and very well behaved, my parents wouldn't have to worry about me and maybe they could work out their differences. I needed to be strong. Hey, a first grader's got to do what a first grader's got to do.

Against this backdrop, finances became even tighter. My dad was a proud man and rather than take unemployment benefits, he chose to take a job as a stock boy for $8 an hour when the unemployment benefits would have paid him more. I even recall my mother telling my brother not to drink so much milk because we couldn't afford it. One time, we were on vacation at Yellowstone. There was a small amusement park called Flintstone Land where you could do such fun activities as ride Barney Rubble's car. While there, my mom bought me a cheap T-shirt. One of my brothers commented, "That's great, Greg, but now we won't have enough money to go home." I believed him rather than realizing he was just teasing me. So, being the dutiful son, I told my parents I was sick and couldn't eat in the hope that the saved money would allow us to all make it back to Utah.

By the time I was eight, I had mastered the art of concealment. I was friendly, sociable, even charismatic. I was tactful and diplomatic. I was helpful and accommodating. I may have been a super nice kid on the outside but inside I felt numb and dumb. I just buried the emotions and sucked it up.

Minivan Therapy

A while later, my parents separated. I did everything I could but I didn't save their marriage. Now that my dad was gone, my mom needed someone to step up and help her at home. My older brothers had either left home or were around only intermittently, so, as I entered junior high school, my mom offered me the role of being the man around the house. I accepted, of course. This role wasn't confined to being helpful physically. My mom wanted me to be her emotional support, too.

Two or three times a week, my mom and I would do minivan therapy. I actually loved the minivan. I remember when we got it. The family finances meant that for the first five years or so of my life we drove around in a beat-up station wagon. I was a little embarrassed to be seen in it if the truth be told, so the maroon minivan with the stripe down the side was a huge upgrade.

Continuing in the minivan tradition that had been established with Dad, my mom would suggest that we go to get an ice cream or a soda. We'd get into the minivan and drive to a local store or the gas station, or sometimes even out of town and she would talk. She would tell me her problems. She would tell me about my dad's problems, although in fairness to her she never really slammed him. She would tell me about our dire financial circumstances. Sometimes she would cry. I was strong and I let her vent. I would listen and eat my ice cream. It might not be what Dr. Phil gets paid for his sessions, but you have to remember that ice cream was a luxury for me. I didn't think there was anything odd or even awkward about these trips. My mom wanted me to go with her, and I was happy to do so.

I was the man of the house for about eighteen months. During that time my sister and I were the prototypical latchkey kids. We'd come home after school and do our own thing. It was pretty solitary even though I joined about every possible group at school, bought lunch with food stamps, and even played football. Not that anyone in my family came to see me play. I wasn't surprised but I was disappointed, not that I showed it. I was cool, diplomatic, and was skating through school in the resource room. I did have great difficulty when I had to read aloud in class. As it got closer for me to read, a red wave of panic filled my mind, making my performance even worse than it was already.

I wanted to be popular but I didn't want anyone to get close to me. If they did, I thought, they would see that I was a fake. I had one really close friend, but as far as everyone else was concerned, my attitude was "please don't find out how stupid I really am." I deflected any of these harsh emotions and accepted the fact that I would amount to nothing. Even the school counselor suggested to me that "college isn't for everyone."

By that time, my mother had started a relationship with another man. Eventually they married and we went to live in his house. I was relieved of my formal duties. But I was forever her rock, her support, the child she could lean on. And I was happy to be that for her. My stepfather was a great guy who provided much-needed financial stability. This allowed my mother to be at home more and we had many, many conversations.

Pizza and Parenthood

When I was a junior in high school, there were two pivotal events that would significantly shape my life. I had been visiting my dad about once a week. He'd gotten into very difficult circumstances after he separated from my mother, but when we went to live with my stepdad, my dad moved back into the family home. My father had been very sick with diabetes. He really didn't take very good care of himself in general and he didn't manage his insulin in particular. He eventually had both kidneys and his pancreas replaced and for a while afterwards was living in a retirement home as it was the only place that he could afford. It was depressing. He was in his early forties and living with people twice his age and looking worse than they did. I could see that he was in decline but felt helpless because I could do nothing about it.

During this time I also got my first job delivering pizzas. I was, of course, reliable, personable, and a good worker. There was a girl working in the same place whose job was to put the toppings on the pizza—and she raised my crust, too. She was actually a year older than I was and she was headed off to college as I started my senior year in high school. I became sexually active, and before long she became pregnant. Well, I might have known how to be the man of the house, but I sure wasn't ready for parenthood. I became a dad two days before my high school graduation. I was seventeen.

We were living separately but sharing the parenting duties. We weren't convinced we were a match made in heaven, so we decided to cease all sexual activity. We almost achieved this completely, but on the one occasion in the fall that we slipped, during a joint babysitting mission, we conceived our second child. We were married by Christmas. We found a small house and cohabitated for a while but were separated within a few months. I moved back in with my mom and stepdad. We were divorced within a few months, and shortly thereafter she moved in with my best friend. He's a great guy and rather than being angry or jealous, I was frankly relieved.

Learning and Losing

Life moved on. I eventually started to address my visual processing problem and realized that I wasn't dumb; rather, I learned differently. I found other ways of learning and actually discovered that my unconventional learning style allowed me to see and solve problems in a different way from most. I still wore the mask and hid myself emotionally but I was beginning to get some confidence.

My mother eventually divorced my stepdad, and I lived with him for a while. As I entered my twenties, I started to see a brighter future for myself. I really embraced the idea of self-improvement and began to study everything

I could. This helped me prepare for the next big event in my life.

In 1999 my father's health really started to decline. He was a great guy. He loved to play the banjo, and when he was healthier he would sit on the front steps of our house and entertain us and anyone else who happened to come by. He could sing for hours. But now his diabetes was so bad that when he cut his foot and it didn't heal, he needed part of his leg amputated. Gangrene had set in and was working its way up his leg. By this time he was on dialysis. Then he fell into a coma.

The family was called to the hospital. We were told that he had probably about a 70 percent chance of surviving the surgery but we should think about whether we wanted them to proceed. We came back the next day only to discover that he had deteriorated and that his chance of survival was now estimated at just 30 percent. My brothers and sister talked about it and decided that the poor man should just be allowed to go to sleep. We agreed that the dialysis machine should be switched off.

A short time later he emerged from his coma. When told of his condition and prospects, he told the doctors that he was worn out and couldn't fight anymore. He, too, asked them to turn off the dialysis machine.

My brothers and sister gathered in his room shortly afterwards. I will never forget it. My older brothers sat on the three sides of his bed; my sister was in a chair nearby. I leaned up against the sink in the back of the room.

My father told us he was proud of us. He told us boys that we were good men. He told us he loved us. My brothers were crying, and my sister was bawling. I wasn't. I was breathing deeply, trying to control my emotions. I guess I didn't want to upset him.

My dad was still alert enough to pick up on what was happening. He looked directly at me as my siblings were wiping their eyes.

"Greg," my dad said, "you don't have to be so strong."

My dad passed away in his sleep that night.

I've often thought about those last words from my father. At the time I thought he was saying to me that it was okay if I showed emotion; he wouldn't be upset. But as I've thought more about his words, I think he was telling me something different, something that transcended his deathbed scene. I think he was telling me that our biggest weaknesses are the overuse of our strengths. Yes, I was strong, but sometimes I needed to let my guard down and feel the emotion.

He was right.

My parents really did their best, and directly or otherwise they taught me a lot. The way I coped with the situations I faced as a child may have created some problems for me, but on the other hand, in some surprising ways, they also prepared me for my roles as husband and father.

#

In the Rearview Mirror: Life Lessons from My Journey

- Your childhood experiences can contribute to how you view relationships as an adult. Consciously and unconsciously, we learn roles and behavioral patterns from our parents that inform our social growth and development—both positively and negatively.

- Financial anxiety can have an incredibly detrimental effect on a marriage; in fact, financial problems are generally considered to be one of the top causes of divorce.

- Wearing a "mask" to conceal your emotions and insecurities doesn't prevent them from impacting your inner well-being. You may succeed in convincing other people that you're "fine," but if you don't directly address what's bothering you, you'll feel numb inside—and you'll have difficulty forming genuine relationships. Don't let your ability to stay strong devolve into a weakness that prevents you from connecting with what's truly best for you.

- Unfortunately, shared parenthood of a child doesn't necessarily mean that two people are suited to be in a relationship with each other. In these instances, separation can be a much healthier option than "forcing" a failing partnership.

CHAPTER TWO

Maturity

After my father's death, I decided it was time to make some changes in my life. I was just beginning to have a sense that I could achieve more than cooking pizzas. With two children to support, there was also added pressure to find ways of making more money. There was also another factor. My self-esteem was still about as low as a limbo dancer on Xanax. I didn't think any woman would want to have anything to do with me. I was an academic failure, divorced with two kids. I needed to up my status. So I left the pizza place in search of more dough.

Building a Better Future

I had been referred to a construction company by a friend of mine. I started off in very manual labor, digging footings and foundations. It was very physically demanding but I had a great work ethic and was willing to learn. The money was decent and I gave it everything I had. Soon, I was given more responsibility. I found myself doing a variety of skilled construction-related chores: framing, roofing, carpentry. I found electrical work literally shocking, so I didn't pursue it as vigorously as the other activities. My reputation as a good worker helped me get on the next step of the ladder.

To get on a better financial footing, I became a concrete truck driver. I got my commercial driver's license, but the job didn't just involve driving the truck. I also had to maneuver the truck and extension lines coming from it to deliver concrete into inaccessible places. This is a complicated, dangerous, and stressful process. For example, sometimes you are extending the pipes from the truck over power lines. Wet concrete and high voltage lines don't mix very well, and there have been serious injuries and even some fatalities when the lines collide. Whenever I was doing this, I was always keeping one eye on the weather because storms could produce serious hazards. When the sun went in, my anxiety came out.

The extension lines from the concrete truck were operated by a remote control panel about the size of an iPad. Operating the truck and the remote required skill and a steady hand. One time, for example, we were laying some new foundations for large printing presses in a difficult location. The concrete was literally being poured in from lines extended into the air above the floor. When the line blew, pounds of concrete were shooting through the air at great velocity! It was quite a sight. Thousands of dollars of damage was done to some of the printing presses. We were just lucky that no one was seriously hurt. Notwithstanding this potential disaster, the money was good for someone in his early twenties with no formal education.

Back to Class

I continued to read a lot of self-help books, especially about financial success and opportunities. I especially liked *Think and Grow Rich* and the *Rich Dad, Poor Dad* series. As I read these books, I felt there was more that I could achieve. Intuitively I felt that I could do and be more. I continued to challenge myself. As a result I decided I needed to go back to school. I signed up at ITT

Tech in Salt Lake City to learn computer programming. The technology sector seemed to be thriving and to have a promising future. I wanted to know more.

But going to school significantly reduced my earnings. Eventually, I found a job working in tech support as a Microsoft engineer. The job didn't pay much but I felt I was getting great hands-on experience even as I was going to school. And I remember that during my very first week on the job it snowed really heavily. I recall looking out of the window in a mixture of relief and pride that this would be the first winter I would not have to work outside in the cold. In order to bolster my finances, I also took a job as a bouncer in a country-and-western bar. The job paid fairly well but also provided a much needed social outlet.

I was working really hard. I had school three nights a week from 6-10 p.m., homework, and two jobs. It was tough, but in my first semester I got all As except in the programming class where I was getting Bs and Cs. I was having a hard time understanding some of the concepts using the textbook we were given. So, between semesters I sought out other books and basically taught myself the course in my own way. My confidence started to increase, especially because in my Microsoft support role I was working with large companies (for example, Dell) as they implemented Windows 2000.

The combination of my self-directed class instruction and the practical experience gained in my Microsoft job really proved to be valuable. For the first time in a class setting, I felt I was performing to my abilities. I tore apart a class in visual basics and decided to switch my focus from network administration to programming. It was a struggle financially, though. But soon an opportunity came along that I couldn't resist applying for, even though one requirement was a bachelor's degree and I didn't have one of those yet.

Even though I didn't have the degree, I did have a lot of relevant work experience, and that was decisive. I was hired.

The job involved working for American Express and installing new software in banks that would facilitate the transfer of Amex traveler's checks funds. Nationally, this amounted to about $1 billion a month. Up to this point, banks would hold on to the money from these checks and transfer it to Amex within a few days. The new software enabled the transfer of these funds from the banks to Amex overnight. Obviously, the banks weren't too pleased with this technological advance as it now deprived them of the use of significant funds for a few days or more. One of my roles was to inform the bank about these changes. Needless to say, I had some interesting conversations.

Panic and a Punch-out

The American Express campus in Salt Lake City is huge and has a massive logo emblazoned across its roof. This became an issue on September 11, 2001. I was on the campus the day the attack on the World Trade Center happened. Everyone was in shock, especially because American Express headquarters were located in the Twin Towers. Many of the senior members of the bank were stunned, wondering how their friends and colleagues were faring while the attacks unfolded in Manhattan. American Express employees were killed that day, and I witnessed horror, hysteria, and grief from my colleagues who knew people in the Twin Towers office.

Speculation was rife. Who else was going to be attacked? Clearly this was a deliberate attack on America's financial institutions from the air. Could our campus be next? We could hardly make an easier target because of the huge logo on the roof. Everyone was in a panic.

No attack materialized against American Express; however, the tech bubble was beginning to burst. There were lots of layoffs at the big banks, and this trickled down to my sector, too. As jobs became threatened, everyone felt more vulnerable, and the previous pleasant working environment deteriorated. In fact, it became quite hostile.

Hostility of another sort also played into my next career moves. As I mentioned, I was a bouncer at a club, and one evening a big fight broke out in the parking lot. There must have been a dozen guys really hitting each other hard. Those of us in security (i.e., bouncers), ran to the lot as it was still considered to be part of our property and thus a liability.

I managed to wrestle one guy to the ground and had him pinned. I told him there was no need to continue, I'd let him walk away—he just needed to stop fighting. As he acknowledged his agreement, I felt a rush of air passing my right ear. One of the other combatants had gotten free and smacked the guy I had pinned square in his eye, which was already swollen. Blood spurted out from around his eye and covered my face. The first thing I could think of was the state of this guy's health. Did he have AIDS or some other blood-borne disorder? It took me six months of testing to prove to my satisfaction that I had not been infected.

With my bouncer's career in decline and my programming job no longer fun, a career move seemed in the cards. The stars aligned. I was dating a girl who was a loan processor at a local mortgage company. She was telling me how business was booming, and before long, I was working for the same loan company part-time. In one month, I closed two mortgages and made a lot of money. Suddenly the math made sense. I decided I should focus on dollars and cents rather than algebra.

(Finally!) Finding My Niche

I quit my job and school and took a job full-time at the finance company. This school experience had been very successful. It showed me that I was not dumb and that I had my own ways of learning that worked very well. In high school my GPA was 2.1; in college it was 3.8.

I enjoyed the challenge of working as a loan officer, and within a few months I was doing really well. In one month I actually closed $700,000 in loans. Soon, a company called Option One recruited me to be an account executive for their mortgage portfolio. I set about implementing my own ideas about how to revive the Utah region, which had lagged behind some of the other states. I studied my competitors and adopted some of their tactics and procedures. I also learned how to effectively communicate and motivate the loan processors.

I was in my element and using my strengths. One month I closed more than $12 million in loans! I made more in that one month than I did in an entire year as a concrete truck operator. The money really started to flow but it also created some problems. Money often does.

For one thing, nobody really told me how to keep money. There are a lot of books on making money, but keeping it is just as important. And as far as I'm aware, there aren't any books on what to do when you make disproportionately more money than other member of your family.

At this time I was making probably three times the amount that my entire family of four siblings was earning. I think they saw me as the get-rich-quick-scheme guy, just chasing anything that would make the most dollars. I didn't see it that way. I was evolving, trying out different things. I had spent a good six figures educating myself and finally realizing that I wasn't dumb. I had taken chances. I had worked hard. I now had a good understanding of both money and technology. I had confidence in my abilities.

For a lot of this time, I hadn't really been dating. Despite my progress on the work front, I still had a lot of self-doubt when it came to relationships. I hadn't really let anyone get close. I was still afraid of rejection. My drive to make money was in no small part fueled by the belief that I had to have money to attract attention and, yes, even love.

That was about to change.

# # #

In the Rearview Mirror: Life Lessons from My Journey

- If you aren't happy with the current state of your life, you have two choices: Stick with the status quo and stay dissatisfied or take steps to change what isn't working. (Yes, when you clear away the excuses, it's often that simple.) The latter option might initially be frightening and require hard work, but how others see you—and more importantly, how you see yourself—will improve. People who take the initiative earn respect.

- You don't have to (and in fact, you shouldn't) face your future armed only with your own knowledge and past experiences. The world is full of books, articles, and videos created by people with valuable lessons to teach. By devoting even a small amount of your time to self-improvement, you'll put yourself in a position to identify and take advantage of future opportunities.

• There is more than one way to get an education—and sometimes, experience can trump a transcript. You might not fit the profile of a potential employer's ideal candidate, but don't let that stop you from pursuing an opportunity. Your long shot might just end up becoming a home run.

• When considering (or reconsidering) your future career, play to your strengths. When you do something you're good at and enjoy, you'll be in a position to maximize your potential (and probably your paycheck, too).

• Many people believe that achieving financial stability (and especially prosperity) will solve a lot of their problems—and to some extent, that's true. However, be aware that a larger bank account can come with its own set of special issues. In particular, learning to be responsible with your money can be an unexpected challenge.

CHAPTER 3

Falling In Love

By late 2003 my confidence was continuing to climb. The concern I had about my lovability was still there but that insecurity was offset by the fact that I had plenty of money in the bank and more streaming in on a regular basis. Life was good.

Although I had been dating some up to this point, the relationships were casual, in part because of my self-doubt. But now I was acquiring status. In fact, I had just bought a house, my very own nest. I was actually surprised by the amount of money I was making. Not for the first time or the last, I felt like a bit of an impostor. My coworkers and I were making so much money for doing what I considered to be fairly easy work. Were we really worth this amount of money?

I started to date some of the loan processors—not all at the same time, however. Since we spent a lot of time together at work, it was easy for me to get to know them and ask them out. However, this was a risky strategy. While I might get some extra business if the relationship was going well, I also ran the risk of losing some accounts if the dating wasn't working out. Sure enough, I was faced with this exact situation. I dated one of the loan processors briefly, but when I discontinued the short relationship, the processor withdrew her account. This cost me about $1 million a month in mortgages, and so I decided I needed better boundaries. I made a rule: No more dating loan processors.

Hello, Sarah!

Not long after I made the dating edict, I met a lovely loan processor named Sarah. Sarah really caught my eye. She was sweet, lighthearted, and a hard worker. She was charming and cute—but she was a loan processor and thus off-limits. However, when I heard she had quit her job, you'd better believe that I was quickly calling her to set up a date.

Sarah was truly a sweetheart. There were a couple of other things about Sarah that made her even more appealing.

First, she had the same values as I did as she, too, was part of the Church of Latter Day Saints. Overall, that was a good thing, but it did have one huge downside. The Mormon religion decries sex before marriage, and we stayed true to those principles. But for a couple falling in love, in their mid-twenties, it wasn't easy. I was twenty-eight, and Sarah was three years younger.

Second, Sarah had a family that seemed to be very cohesive. The oldest of four sisters and with an older brother, Sarah seemed to be well integrated into the family life. Unlike my family, in Sarah's there seemed to be little in the way of sibling feuding; everyone seemed to get along well and they enjoyed doing things together.

The more I knew Sarah, the more I felt she was the perfect match for me. Apart from the qualities mentioned above, I thought she could be a great role model and would teach me a lot. Besides, unlike me, she hadn't been married before. She made me feel good. It was obvious we were falling in love.

Romantic love is obviously a phase designed to get people to pair up in order to procreate. The attachment and sexual urgency color perceptions during this phase; your partner is perfect and can do no wrong, and she feels the same about you.

The dynamic worked for us. In her family, Sarah was the caregiver, the "good girl" who could always be counted on, the hard worker, the reliable one. I, too, was the caregiver, the superhero, there to make sure everyone was okay. I could fix other people's problems by being there and being kind, and so could Sarah. It seemed like a match made in heaven, but the seeds of destruction were also sown.

On the Fast Track

We had a blast during our courtship. We blew through a lot of money doing some fun things. It wasn't that we spent thousands of dollars doing really lavish activities; more that we enjoyed some of the finer things in life: food, clothing, wine, and entertainment. We went to some of the best restaurants, like the Sundance Tree Room restaurant. This is a spectacular venue that features a huge, live tree in the middle of the dining area. The food is exceptional, and the wine is expensive. Dinner for two can easily set you back a few hundred bucks, but we loved every minute of eating out and sparing no expense.

I also instituted the "FedEx Prize," which was a gift delivered by FedEx. These gifts weren't just delivered to our homes; they could be delivered anywhere. For instance, during a visit to Las Vegas, I arranged for a Louis Vuitton purse to be delivered to the hotel as a gift for my lovely girlfriend.

We were having a blast. By September 2004, after nine months of fun, fascination, and frustration, we were engaged. This was the woman I wanted to spend the rest of my life with.

After a lot of discussion, we decided that we wanted to get married at the Mormon Temple in Oahu, Hawaii, which is close to the famous Turtle Bay Resort. We started to look at possible dates in the early part of 2005, about six months in the future.

The Turtle Bay Resort is home to many activities: golf, surfing, tennis, hiking, fitness, and many other options for the active person. The resort also hosts some major events and tournaments, and as we looked at the calendar we found that all the dates we were considering for the early part of 2005 were unavailable. We didn't want to have to wait too long to marry, so we started to entertain the idea of getting married sooner. The best available time from the resort's perspective was early December. There was just one problem: Sarah's sister was to be married just three days earlier.

Sarah's second-youngest sister was just 19. She had met a guy who was considerably older and had a daughter from a previous marriage. Undeterred, my future father-in-law had spent a decent amount on the wedding. He was not too thrilled at the prospect of a second wedding just three days later.

Being the guy who wants to make everything right and ensure everyone feels okay, I offered to cover our costs in Hawaii and to fly my future in-laws out to Hawaii, too. Sarah's mother was ambivalent at first but eventually agreed. The arrangements were made, and early December came upon us fast. Before you could say, "I do," we were on the plane headed west.

When we finally got to the resort, I checked in with my father-in-law. The hotel clerk told us that she could give us our rooms but that they would be five rooms apart. She asked if that would be okay.

"No," my father-in-law insisted, "we need them to be adjoining rooms."

I cringed. Remember, Sarah and I had yet to consummate our relationship, and the prospect of my in-laws being within earshot of my room was making me very uncomfortable, to say the least.

When my father-in-law saw the look on my face, he burst out laughing. He "got me good," as they say. As we all checked into our rooms, I was relieved to see that they were far enough apart for my satisfaction.

The schedule was tight. As it turned out, we had only a couple of hours to get a marriage license and then rush to the temple for the ceremony. As I entered the temple, a crusty local stopped me and asked, "Are you sure you want to do this? This is your last chance to leave."

I didn't leave. My in-laws did leave after a few days, and Sarah and I stayed on to have a wonderful time. We rented a burgundy Chrysler PT convertible and cruised around Oahu. (You can actually drive the whole island in about three hours.) We had fun stopping at small stalls that sold pineapple and getting instant refreshment. We did the same with coconuts, but once was enough for me. The coconut was cut open and a straw inserted. I was expecting a cool, sweet elixir, but it was anything but. We ate at shrimp shacks and fine restaurants. We hung out on the beach, and I snorkeled. It was everything you hope a honeymoon would be.

Trouble in Paradise

We returned to Utah to settle in to married bliss. The only problem was that, like many newly married couples, we didn't think through our vision for married life. We didn't consider what we needed as people in the short- and long-term. We just focused on the money and the lifestyle.

One of the first decisions we made was that Sarah no longer needed to work. She could be a stay-at-home mom. The only problem was that we didn't have any kids yet. And I don't think either of us realized there was more value to Sarah's working than just the money she was earning. She was an excellent worker who got a lot of approval from colleagues, and she enjoyed positive social interaction at work that would be hard to replicate at home. While staying at home and hanging out with her mom seemed like more fun initially, this decision ended up being unhealthy for Sarah.

All of us have roles we play in our families, and it is difficult to escape them when surrounded by that same family. In her own family, Sarah was the responsible one and the caregiver, often to the detriment of her own needs. It would be difficult for her to forge a different identity while spending a lot of time in her nuclear family, all of whom expected her to play her usual role. Neither of us realized this at the time, though. Instead of having children, we bought two Havanese dogs, Bentley and Bugatti, that Sarah could take care of in her more than ample free time.

Sarah seemingly had everything any young woman could wish for but appeared depressed and anxious. Her sleep started to suffer. We were two years into our marriage. Sarah was unfulfilled, and I was overwhelmed and immersed in my work. Moreover, being the "superhero," I just wanted to make it better for Sarah. But instead of confronting our issues head on, I indulged her even more.

Then we got pregnant with our daughter, Ella. It was 2006 and my business was fluctuating. Money ebbed and flowed, and now, faced with a new addition to the family, I was stressing out. But I didn't want to burden Sarah with these concerns. I wanted to protect her so I struggled on alone. Because of the demands of my business and the approach to my marriage, I never felt I achieved a proper balance. I was always thinking about work and taking on everything I could at home. We were both unfulfilled even after Ella was born.

We avoided the real issues by putting our energies into other ventures. We bought a new home, an upgrade on our existing one, and that gave us something to talk about and work on together. But it was an escape.

Now, three years, a child, and two dogs into our marriage, we were both frustrated. I know that I still loved Sarah very much, but in playing our classic roles, each of us failed to address the core issues. For one, I realize that I was still playing the negotiator, trying to make it work but not addressing the real problems. I needed to be more of a leader than a negotiator. I needed to step up and lead us to serious assessment of our relationship, our goals, and our lives. Instead, that discussion dropped by the wayside by default, and dissatisfaction continued to burrow its way into our marriage.

Part of the problem was that divisions were occurring in my wife's family, and, of course, from my perspective it seemed that Sarah was charged with fixing all the problems. This conflict didn't help Sarah's disposition or our relationship.

The distance between us increased. By our natures, neither of us is a big fighter, so there wasn't that much drama; but on the other hand, there just wasn't much of anything: progress, intimacy, or contentment. So we decided we would make things better by getting pregnant again!

I enjoyed being a dad. Every night I would come home and spend time with Ella, but that was the problem: It was just me and Ella. There never seemed time for family bonding, to create and nurture ourselves as a family. I would take over to "relieve" Sarah of parental duties, but we needed time together.

A Move in the Wrong Direction

In 2009, as we were expecting Mattis, we made another spectacular decision. We decided to lease a huge mansion that was big enough to accommodate my in-laws. The place, set high up on a hill with gorgeous views, was about 10,000 square feet with a massive space for my in-laws—but space wasn't the issue.

I had spent a lot of time with my father-in-law since my marriage; we were business partners in a variety of ventures, and generally I had a good relationship with him. But in retrospect, as I've said, I believe that Sarah was trapped in the same old family dynamic. It's nobody's fault, but I just think children shouldn't live with their parents as adults since it prevents them from growing into new roles and developing as people.

Instead of bringing my in-laws into our home, we should have been putting more distance between us. Again, this is nothing to do with my in-laws as people. I just don't think that dynamic works, period. Young adults need to be independent so that they can find their own ways and build their own families.

Tension started to run high even after Mattis was born. There was conflict as well as concerns about money. When the lease was up on the mansion after a year, we downgraded and ended the experiment in communal living.

Looking back on these years, I think that "life" ran us, not the other way around. We didn't pay attention to our personal needs. Sure, we had occasional date nights, but then it was back to the same old grind. Yes, we went to church on Sunday and did all the things you're supposed to do, but we were checking off obligations rather than living in the moment. Sarah was becoming more and more isolated. I was becoming more frustrated.

In his book *The Five Love Languages*, Gary Chapman identifies the various ways that people receive and give love. The gifts are: physical touch, gifts, service, time, and appreciation. Initially, I was able to provide Sarah with some lavish gifts, but there were times when I couldn't sustain that level of spending. Equally, one of the ways I like to be loved is through appreciation, and that became more difficult for her to provide.

I recall one time when I returned from a long weekend workshop on self-help and development. I was pumped. I wanted to share it with my wife, but she wasn't very interested. Perhaps I was expecting too much. She couldn't have been as excited—she wasn't there. I was deflated. Would we ever really connect?

These disconnects continued to drive us apart. Neither of us had evolved. We hadn't matured out of our family roles and that kept us stuck. Ultimately, it was our undoing.

During a discussion in 2010, I told her that I was staying married only for the sake of the children. Looking back I think we still had the potential to love one another. We just didn't know how to do it. When we moved out of the honeymoon phase (as everyone does after a few months), we didn't have the tools or the direction to continue our development as a team committed to nurturing our family and each other.

Now we faced a big decision.

# # #

In the Rearview Mirror: Life Lessons from My Journey

- This cliché bears repeating: Be very careful when dating coworkers! Once you become romantic, business isn't just business any longer: It will *always* be personal.

- The "honeymoon phase" of a relationship is blissful but can also be deceptive. In the throes of attraction and infatuation, it's easy for new couples to overlook incompatibilities and make self-indulgent decisions while ignoring their implications for the future. When beginning a relationship, try to stay aware of the longer-term consequences your decisions might have on your emotions and finances.

- Don't underestimate the impact fulfilling work can have on your happiness. While you might not enjoy every aspect of your work, the sense of purpose, accomplishment, and social connection you get from your job might be more valuable than you realize.

- As you grow, change, and develop as an individual, it can be challenging to reconcile the "new you" to the person your family and friends expect you to be. (For instance, family members may still see and treat you as a child well into adulthood.) Even if it's initially uncomfortable, you may need to be lovingly assertive in negotiating new roles and dynamics that are healthy for you.

- You may keep your worries, problems, and anxieties from your partner in order to avoid burdening him or her, or to avoid uncomfortable confrontation. But don't fool yourself—you aren't doing your partner any favors. A large degree of openness and honesty (about the good, the bad, *and* the ugly) is essential to maintaining a healthy, trusting, and fulfilling relationship. Plus, you may be surprised by the support, and maybe even solutions, your partner is able to provide.

• There's no external solution to fixing core issues in a marriage. Distracting yourselves with a vacation, a new car, a new house, and even a new child won't stave off the real problems for long.

• In our hectic, overscheduled world, it's easy to get the message that focusing on yourself is selfish. It isn't. In fact, investing time and energy in yourself and in your close relationships is an essential part of maintaining your physical, mental, and emotional health.

CHAPTER FOUR

Parenting

I was not ready to be a parent at seventeen. It was not that I didn't try and wasn't responsible. By and large, I was and I gave my best. But being such a young dad when I was still trying to work out who I was myself was scary and stressful.

Remember, in my late teens and early twenties I was still struggling with my self-esteem. I didn't think I was very smart and I wasn't sure how I was going to make money. This was a huge issue as I was very mindful of my child support obligations. Having children at such a young age really gets you to confront the realities of life, especially about work and money. You have mouths to feed. Responsibility beckons.

Aaron and Taylor, my children from my first marriage to Sally, were great kids. After our divorce, I got to see them every other weekend and occasionally during the middle of the week. I wanted to see them as much as possible and I did. However, I also had to make as much money as I could, and this required eventually working two jobs. So sometimes, when the kids would come over on the weekend, I would be with them until early evening, and then my mother would take over when I went off to my job at the club. I would arrive home at three in the morning and then make sure I was awake when the children woke up, so I could spend as much time as possible with them.

What really helped this situation was that my ex's new husband, Ryan, was a friend of mine. I had known him long before I met Sally and I was very comfortable with him being the stepdad of my children. Very comfortable, indeed. So there was no conflict between the three parents involved, which I am sure made a huge difference to the children. I'm not saying that we were completely in sync on every single aspect of parenting, but we were free of the nastiness and divisiveness that accompanies many divorces and that many children of divorce have to endure. I am sure that peace and security are essential for children, and that a stable, safe home with one parent is better than a war zone with two.

Dad on a Date

My status as a divorced dad with two children did have a major effect on one specific area of my personal life. When I was dating, I wrestled with the question of whether and when I should tell my dates that I was a divorced father of two. After all, I was barely in my twenties, and this is not a common situation. I decided that in the initial stages of a potential relationship (i.e., the first couple of dates), it wasn't necessary to tell my dates about my status. I thought this was really too much information and that it didn't need to be shared. Besides, I am sure many of these dates themselves had relevant personal information that they didn't share early on in a relationship, cither. So I was comfortable with the decision to delay telling my girlfriends about my children until it seemed necessary.

This decision had absolutely nothing to do with my children. I just wanted to see how any relationship would develop first, without my status influencing the progress of our friendship. Once we had been on a few dates and it looked like we might be more than just people who would occasionally hang out together, I would come clean about my status.

Coming clean about the fact that I was divorced and had two children was always a difficult and stressful time for me. I would typically tell my girlfriend about it and then wait for the reaction. That reaction typically wouldn't be very revealing at the time I told her. I knew I would get my real answer within the next 72 hours. Would she respond to my calls or blow me off? These were the days before texting and there were several times I recall waiting nervously to find out the reaction of my "girlfriend." Some of them indeed never contacted me again, but for others my status didn't seem to make much, or any, difference.

This situation could, however, lead to awkwardness or downright embarrassment. I recall one time when a girl I had just started dating called my house. The phone was answered by my stepdad. When the girl asked for me, my stepdad replied, "Can you just hold on—I think he's changing his daughter's diaper at the moment." Click.

The truth was that while almost everyone my age was going to bars and drinking beer, I was often at home making formula or changing diapers.

When it was my weekend to have the children, I wouldn't socialize. I would go to work and then be home for them, unless I was working a second job. These weekend "gaps" also were difficult to explain to girls, too, which is another reason for coming clean as soon as possible. Most people my age lived for the weekend, a time to go and have a lot of fun. It must have seemed odd when I, the fun-loving guy, dropped out every other weekend.

There was one issue with my children that I had not expected. Aaron and Taylor had my last name, but when Sally married Ryan, she took his. This name mismatch alerted everyone that Aaron and Taylor were children of divorce. This seemed to be brought up way too much and certainly more than I ever realized. When there's a surname mismatch with mom, the assumption from school administrators, teachers, friends, doctors, nurses—pretty much whomever you meet—is that the children are from a broken home. Then this becomes the topic of conversation. The children become easily identified by their "product of divorce" status. I really didn't like that, and it was something that influenced my future thinking.

I played a significant role in my kids' lives as I was finding out more about mine. One of the lessons I learned along the way was that parents need to teach children important life lessons. In retrospect, I didn't know those life lessons myself in my late teens and early twenties, so I couldn't have known how to pass them on to my children. But later, as I learned about life, I was determined to provide my children with the important principles of life.

Around the time Sarah and I were married, Sally, Ryan, Aaron, and Taylor moved to Arizona. Aaron was eleven at the time, and Taylor was nine. Suddenly, the time with my children was drastically reduced. Yes, I had them longer in the summer, but my involvement in their everyday lives was effectively eliminated. Sure, I called them regularly, but it was not the same as playing video games, having dinner with them, or just being there on a regular basis.

Parenthood: Take Two

It wasn't long after Aaron and Taylor moved to Arizona that Sarah and I learned we were expecting Ella. It had been twelve years since I'd had my first child, Aaron, and I had learned a lot. By this time (2006), I had a much better sense of who I was as a person—my strengths, weaknesses, goals, and aspirations. I had developed some self-confidence. I had learned some valuable lessons.

I had learned that we all have talents and gifts. I had learned that many people will tell you that you can't do something when you really can. I had learned the power of being positive, of hard work, of self-discipline. These were the lessons I wanted to teach my children, and I was now able to do so because I had learned them myself.

I also realized as I became a parent again that parenting isn't a role you can do by default. Parenting needs to be conscious and considered. Parents need to provide safety and security for their children, and this is achieved through structure. In my household, that structure came through routines, which had meaning because they taught important lessons.

Routine, Structure, and Self-Esteem

Around this time I became familiar with the Marshmallow Test. This study, conducted by Stanford University psychologist Walter Mischel in the 1960s and 1970s, used nursery school children to test the value of impulse control. In the study, children were brought into the experiment room where they were exposed to a marshmallow, cookie, or other treat. They were told they could eat the marshmallow immediately, or wait a few minutes—at which point they could get a second marshmallow if the first was still uneaten. Essentially, it was an experiment in delaying immediate gratification for greater rewards.

The subjects in this study were followed for decades. The results were clear: The children who delayed gratification for greater rewards had better life outcomes as measured by higher SAT scores, educational attainment, body-mass index (BMI), and other life measures, than those who ate the marshmallow immediately.

The ability to delay gratification seemed very important to me. I determined that was a crucial life lesson that I would teach my children. I wanted to prepare them for success and give them strategies and mindsets that would allow them to be their best. And if they could be their best, I was fairly sure they would also be happy.

So, from an early age, both Ella, and then her brother, Mattis, were given the expectation that they were part of a team and had to contribute. That might mean putting their toys away or bringing their dishes to the sink, but the expectation was that they would do their share.

These activities were reinforced through routine and repetition. We were consistent in expecting the children to do the same thing every time. I know it's easy at times to do the children's chores for them. You put the toys away and take their dishes to the sink. The problem is that changes their expectations, and they think that they no longer have to do the task in question. I found that consistency was key for the child's own sense of contribution, and that it also reinforced security, since the child knew that the rules didn't change.

Moreover, as my confidence grew, I was able to act with more courage about my convictions. This enabled me to stand firm and stick to the established rules. Honestly, I think this made life easier for my children.

For example, when Ella was scheduled to go to kindergarten, she was considered to be a little behind where she needed to be with her reading. I could relate to that. One option was for her to repeat her pre-K year so she would be more prepared when she finally got to kindergarten.

Knowing the struggles that I'd had because I was behind my peers and how much damage that did to my psyche, I firmly believed that it was in Ella's best interests to repeat her pre-K year. The school was okay with this, but a sister-in-law who was a substitute teacher argued against me and tried vehemently to change my mind. Honestly, I resented her intrusion and I stuck to my guns, something I might not have done earlier in my life.

Ella did indeed stay back one year and had caught up by the time she got to kindergarten. In fact, she progressed so well that within a couple of years she had been accelerated ahead a year and caught up with her age group. I am so glad I stood firm.

I always wanted my children to have fun but never sacrificed routines and structure. For example, Ella and Mattis used to love to snuggle up with me in my big bed to watch movies. But they always went back to their own beds to sleep. Believe me, it would have been easier to let them sleep in the big bed but that would have given the wrong message. And when Sarah and I separated (which I'll talk about in the next chapter), I wanted to preserve the children's routines as much as possible. I would pick Ella up and take her to school every day.

I also wanted to allow my children to be themselves and not feel intimidated by anyone or anything. So we would do fun things that built self-esteem. For example, we would sing as we grocery shopped. We weren't annoying, and most people gave us big smiles when they could see the fun we were having. I didn't want my children to be inhibited, and I did want them to have fun. (And I actually think they learned some valuable things about public speaking and public presentation!)

I also instituted a system where my children were rewarded for delaying gratification and saving, as in the Stanford Marshmallow Study. The children got small amounts of money for doing chores, but the more they saved, the more valuable the rewards became. They could earn about a dollar a weekend. They could spend it or they could trade $10 in for something special that was worth a lot more than $10. If they saved $40, which might take them the best part of a year, they could trade that in for a big trip, like to Disneyland.

By the time I was separated from Sarah, I was making good money. It would have been easy to have been the "Disneyland Dad" and indulge my children. But that would have been disrespectful to my ex and it would have hurt my children in the long run. That didn't mean I didn't do special things with my children, but they were typically adventures on which they learned valuable lessons.

For instance, I once organized a photo shoot for Ella with a professional photographer. Was this an indulgence? No, not really. Ella learned the value of patience and the need to take directions that day. The shoot lasted four hours, during which Ella was asked to adopt various poses, hold them for what seemed like minutes, and then redo the whole thing again and again.

These principles and practices were very important to me, and they have been the backbone of maintaining my kids' self-esteem and security during the most difficult time for any child—their parents' divorce.

#

In the Rearview Mirror: Life Lessons from My Journey

- By using "product of divorce" as a term to describe children, we do them a disservice and cause others to make (often unfair) assumptions about them and their parents. Peace and security are essential for children, and a stable, safe home with one parent is better than a war zone with two.

- Your children may not always listen to you, but it's still important to share as many life lessons as you can with them—especially lessons that you yourself have learned in the School of Hard Knocks! Good parenting isn't something you can do by default, so it's important to put conscious consideration into what you're teaching through your words and actions.

- If you have children, it's inevitable that some people will disagree with your parenting methods. It's wise to take their criticism and suggestions into account, but don't let others sway you from doing what you believe is best for your family. Every situation and every child is different.

- Enforcing rules, routines, and structures can make you feel like the bad guy at times, but standing firm is to your children's benefit. This is especially important to keep in mind if you're separated or divorced. If each parent has a different set of rules and standards, frustration for everyone (adults *and* kids) will be increased.

CHAPTER FIVE

Things Fall Apart

As I've described, Sarah and I began drifting in our marriage as time went by. We were stagnating and disconnected, and I didn't know how to get us back on track. It wasn't that we hated each other, far from it. We just weren't connected. Our marriage had begun to feel a bit like living with a roommate but with many more obligations.

I am sure many couples reach this stage in their relationships. They begin to circle in their own orbits and have less and less in common, or seem to. For many people, that's when the grass starts to look greener. That's when they imagine a different and better marriage. That's when trouble can really take hold.

In all honesty, even though I was not happy, I didn't have many thoughts about the alternative lives I could be living. For me, it was more a sense that the marriage wasn't working and was holding us back as people. We weren't growing, and that's what was bothering me the most.

A Difficult Subject

One of the difficulties in this situation is, how do you address this subject? And once you've done that, how do you talk about it productively? Unlike some couples, we were never ones to throw the "D" word around. I have always felt that talking about divorce whenever anything went wrong was very disrespectful, very negative, and obviously combative. How can threatening divorce be an effective communication strategy? It might intimidate a partner, or strike fear into him or her, but that's hardly a basis for building a better relationship. And the more you talk about divorce, the more it is likely to happen. It's completely the wrong focus *if* you genuinely want to stay together.

I understand that conflict can lead to reconciliation, and in that post-conflict resolution, positive feelings can arise, leading to temporary closeness. Unless you deal with the underlying issues, however, that closeness will be temporary. This happened to us.

One night I sat Sarah down and expressed openly how frustrated I was that we were not close and had drifted so far apart. This wasn't a surprise to her, but she took it seriously. The "D" word wasn't mentioned, and our conversation did elicit some genuine warmth between us. We vowed to try harder. It lasted a couple of weeks.

Having made the effort, felt some closeness, and then lost it again, our problems were even more evident. Soon enough we were having another of those conversations, and this time I stated for the first time that I was staying in the marriage only because of the children.

Sarah was shocked and hurt, though neither of those feelings were my intention. But if we weren't moving forward, there surely wasn't any going back. Before long, we were talking earnestly about separation. In fact, I think I came to accept that reality before Sarah could really come to grips with it.

When it became clear that separation was a dawning reality, I really made a conscious decision about what I wanted and how I was going to conduct myself through what would surely be a difficult time for me, Sarah, and the kids, too.

Soul Searching

What did I want?

Fortunately, what I wanted wasn't the furniture, a car, or the flat screen TV. I didn't want to hurt my wife and I didn't want to win. What I wanted was for our separation to be as painless as possible for everyone. I wanted my children to feel love and be secure. I wanted my wife to feel loved and as secure as she could be in this situation. How could I achieve this?

The more I thought about it, the more one word kept popping up in my head. Consistency. Love is based on trust, and trust is based on consistency. If I was consistent in my words and deeds, Sarah and my children could trust me.

I also realized that I needed to take responsibility for my obligations. I needed to be responsible and consistent in my financial obligations, and in my time and other commitments.

In addition to responsibility and consistency, I wanted my children to feel safe and secure. And that meant changing as little as possible in their lives.

These principles provided a great road map for me during my separation and, ultimately, our divorce. It wasn't always easy, but I stuck with them, and it made a huge difference to all of us, who after all, were still a family.

The Peanut Gallery

One of the problems in this situation is other people. Everyone has their opinions, which are almost certainly not based on facts but others' anxieties, projections, and biases. Let's face it, your friends are going to support you, and her friends are going to support her. Her family will support her; yours will support you. I soon decided that what other people thought and said didn't matter. They weren't unbiased, fully informed observers but people with their own allegiances. They were entitled to whatever opinion they had; I just didn't care about it. Moreover, Sarah needed her family's support, so I didn't want to get in the way of it.

To be honest, the decision not to respond to others' views or care about their opinions saved me an enormous amount of time and energy. It also saved any unnecessary conflict with Sarah. I'm sure her family had strong opinions about me and my actions but I just wasn't going to engage.

Parenting through a Divorce

My overall position was helped by another decision I made. I tried to put myself in Sarah's position. I knew that Sarah had never been divorced, and she had certainly never divorced me before. I am sure she was scared. And I also realized that if I could make it as easy as possible for her, a lot of potential damage, damage that would affect everyone, could be avoided. I was helped in this view by having a long-term focus. Yes, I knew there would be strains and tensions through the transition period, but my focus was much greater than that.

Sarah and I had children together and hopefully would be spending time together in our roles as parents. I didn't want to give Sarah any grounds for bad-mouthing me to the children, since it was important to me that I preserve and develop my relationship with them. I wanted Sarah to have a great relationship with them, too. I realized that all of these goals were achievable if I remained caring, consistent, and responsible.

I moved out and for a week or so lived in a hotel that was about five miles away. This allowed me to continue to be involved in my children's lives in exactly the same way I had been before the separation. I continued to take Ella to school every day. I made sure I was at home to play with them and to put them to bed. If anything, my schedule became even more consistent than it had been before. Previously, I might finish work at

5:00, or I might not get home until 7:30. Now I was "home" at the same time every day. If I thought I was going to be even a couple of minutes late, I would text to say I was on my way.

In an effort to ensure as little as possible changed for my children, I took nothing from the house except my clothes. There was plenty I could have taken once I found myself a place to stay. We had three living room sets and multiple TVs but I left all of that at home. I didn't want to take things; I wanted to share the love.

Sarah and I worked out a visitation schedule that had me with the kids two days every week. Sarah also knew that, within reason, if she needed anything, I would be there. But I was also mindful of not being there *too* much. Sarah needed to adapt to her new reality. New boundaries needed to be established.

Over the next few months, we worked out the details of our divorce agreement. We needed an attorney only to take it before a judge to be ratified.

Moving On

The next hurdle in the divorce process typically comes when one and/or both former partners start dating other people. It was a few months before Sarah informed she was dating. I was pleased for her. Again, I made a conscious decision. This time it was the decision to avoid the two Js: judgment and jealousy. I knew that Sarah was responsible and wouldn't do anything to affect the children. This was her journey, and I wanted to be as supportive as possible of her. It was interesting when she confided in me things about her relationship. Ironically, we were talking about some of the issues that we hadn't been able to discuss during our marriage.

A few months later, Sarah had broken up with her first post-marriage boyfriend and was dating a man named Trevor. Trevor lived about sixty miles away, and it wasn't long before he was spending a lot of time at the house. It wasn't too much longer before he moved in.

Trevor was an entrepreneur and definitely into self-improvement. I was happy to see that this was having a positive influence on Sarah. In fact, she seemed to be really growing personally, which I was thrilled about. I hadn't been able to nurture her in that way and I was so happy that she was now making great strides and developing in the way she needed. During a conversation around this time, she admitted that she "created situations in which [I] couldn't win."

Sarah was referring to the fact that during our time together she had very set expectations, not just of me but everybody. This led me to feel that I could never do anything right, that I'd never understand her criteria or the rules that guided her judgments and feelings. This is a huge stumbling block in any relationship or marriage. Actually, any meaningful relationship isn't about being right; it's about being understanding, nurturing, and loving. If you insist on being right, there's a good chance you're going to be left alone.

Trevor was the beneficiary of Sarah's insight and development. He clearly provided a great loving relationship in which she could thrive. I was thinking about these issues and musing whether I should sit down with Trevor and share my thoughts with him. Intuition told me to contact him, so I texted him and asked if he would like to meet for coffee. He replied, saying he had likewise been thinking of asking me to meet. I wasn't sure whether he was going to tell me that he and Sarah were going to separate or get married, but I was fairly sure it was one or the other.

Meeting the New Guy...and the Facebook Post That Inspired This Book

When we did meet, Trevor told me that they were planning to get married but wanted to talk to me first. I don't think he was asking permission but looking for some clarity about our relationship and my feelings.

We spent two hours talking about a lot of very important things. I told him the three things that I wished I had done differently that might have made a difference in my marriage.

- I told him that I wished I had been a stronger leader in the family instead of letting my relationship with Sarah develop (or not) by default.

- I told him I wished we had moved away from Sarah's family, which would have taken pressure off of her and would probably have allowed us to grow together.

- I also volunteered that I probably should have been a better financial manager and stronger in maintaining the family budget.

Trevor told me he had been divorced but had no children. He asked me point blank whether I had any reservations about his being the kids' stepdad. I really didn't. It was clear that we shared the same values and wanted the same things.

The time we spent together was a real bonding experience. I really appreciated that I got to talk to him face-to-face and not have a conversation indirectly through Sarah. It set the tone for the future.

In that future, I have no problem with my children calling Trevor "dad." Why should I? I don't feel replaced by him and I am very happy that my kids have such a cool guy in their lives. He has accepted the responsibility of that role and it only makes my children more secure. Once in a while, we will all do things together. For example, we had a blast at Easter, and I think it was good for the kids to see that all the significant adults in their lives can get along well.

Setting the right boundaries and expectations was appropriate and critical during our separation and divorce and it continues to be now that Sarah is remarried. For example, she is not part of my social media network. However, that didn't stop me from posting a photo of the two of us on Facebook when I heard she was getting married.

The message read:

My ex-wife is cooler than your ex-wife.

I am so proud of her.

Not only is she

An amazing mom

Funny

Beautiful

Caring

And smart

This girl finally set her wedding date to an amazing guy!

I could not be more proud and happy for someone!

I love them both.

And I meant every word.

#

In the Rearview Mirror: Life Lessons from My Journey

- Whether you feel that the grass might be greener somewhere else or are simply ambivalent about your spouse, treat a disconnected marriage as the red flag it is. There don't necessarily need to be arguments and fights for a marriage to be in trouble.

- While it's fine to talk about divorce if you and your spouse genuinely feel that going your separate ways might be better for both of you, don't use the "D-word" frivolously or as a threat. This introduces fear, intimidation, and combativeness into the conversation, which is in no way productive. And the more you consider divorce as an option (even if you aren't very serious at first), the more likely it is to happen.

- Mutual acknowledgment that there are problems in a marriage is a good start, but it isn't enough. If you don't do the difficult work of addressing the issues in your relationship head-on, any temporary closeness you feel will soon wear off—and you'll be back to square one.

- It's easy (and sometimes tempting) to make a separation or divorce all about "me, me, me." But unless your spouse is threatening or combative, take a step back and think about how to make this difficult time as painless as possible for everyone involved (especially for your children, if you have them). Maintaining consistency and trust are great goals by which to steer your course. And striving to keep a long-term focus instead of zeroing in on short-term inconveniences and frustrations will help you to keep the transition period from becoming more acrimonious than it needs to be.

- When you're going through a divorce, remind yourself that "the peanut gallery" may have a lot of opinions and criticisms, but they almost certainly don't have all the facts. Try not to become too stressed or anxious because of how other people think you should be living *your* life.

- Believe it or not, there are pitfalls unique to amicable divorces. If you and your ex continue to be present in one another's lives (which is especially likely if you have children), you may not be giving each other enough space to truly move on. Be mindful of the dangers of not changing your routines and roles enough!

- After a divorce, be wary of allowing the two Js (jealousy and judgment) to creep into your life once your former partner begins to move on. It may be difficult to see your ex with another person, but remember, you no longer have a claim and you (presumably) want the best for him or her!

- A divorce is a great opportunity to reevaluate your life, attitudes, and behaviors—particularly in regard to how they impact your relationships. What has your failed marriage taught you about yourself, your spouse, and what you want for the future? What would you do differently, given a second chance? Depending on your relationship, you may even find it helpful to discuss these things with your ex and/or your new partners.

CHAPTER SIX

The 9 Reasons
for Being "Selfish"

My decision to continue to be loving toward my ex-wife has handsomely rewarded all involved by creating better lives not just for her but also for me and my children. There have been so many benefits of taking a caring, understanding position as opposed to an adversarial one. My children are happy, and there is no discomfort or awkwardness when they are with me and/or when they are with me, my ex, and their stepfather, Trevor. This is a relief for everyone. My ex and I have a direct line of communication and can talk openly and honestly. Moreover, I think that both Sarah and I have no regrets about how we handled our divorce and our subsequent actions.

While it might look like I have just taken the moral high ground for the sake of it, the fact is that, apart from feeling that my approach is the "right" way to deal with divorce from a moral perspective, it actually has some very significant practical benefits in both the short-term and the long-term. In short, doing the right thing also turned out to be an act of selfishness. Not selfish in the narcissistic sense, but selfish in the sense of *taking care* of myself. And part of taking care of myself was also taking care of Sarah and the children. Their care and well-being were important to me, so I was self-serving but in a way that helped all of us.

Nine Benefits of Being "Selfish" During a Divorce

The benefits of taking the high ground and having a "selfish" divorce certainly aren't limited to my experiences; I believe they're available to everyone. So if you aren't sure that being selfish as I define it is worth your while, read the following list I've put together and see if your experience changes.

These nine benefits of a selfish divorce aren't listed in any particular order (certainly not in the order of their importance for me personally). However, I think for many people, especially in the heat of a failing marriage, practical considerations seem paramount, and that's why I have presented them in this order.

1. Taking the high ground helps you save money.

Attorneys are expensive. And if you have children and get into a protracted custody battle, the bills can be astronomical. I know people who have spent more than $200,000 fighting in court over custody and support issues. That is criminal. That money could have gone a long way toward their three children's education. It actually had a very significant negative impact on the children they were fighting over. (So much for acting in the best interests of your children!) Also, a protracted court case is stressful. Stress leads to health issues, and health issues lead to health professionals who need to be paid. There are so many ways that an adversarial approach costs money. It's not just the attorneys and the court assessors and the guardians ad litem; it's time off work, professional assessments, therapy, etc.

2. Being "selfish" enables you to conserve energy and time.

A domestic breakup is hard for everybody. It involves change and attention to details; there is a lot to do as you settle into a new lifestyle and perhaps even find a new place to live. Managing this change takes energy. You have only so much energy and a lot of it can be spent in arguing, fighting, and positioning yourself, not to mention time spent with attorneys and in court. The same could be said about time. After I had amicably resolved my situation with my ex, my productivity and revenue increased 25 percent in the next two months. With my domestic situation taken care of in a way I felt good about, I could redevote pretty much all my energy to my business, and that paid immediate dividends.

3. An amicable divorce cuts down on stress.

The longer your divorce or separation takes, the more stressful it is. And don't underestimate the impact of stress. It affects energy as described above, not to mention the related variables of sleep and health. Prolonged stress reduces your immune system's ability to keep your body healthy. It's not just the diseases that people think of as stress-induced, like heart disease or ulcers, that increase under chronic stress; it's anything and everything. Prolonged stress will really enhance the chances of getting sick, and it will definitely get you off your game. This is an important consideration, especially if you are facing or considering a long-term custody battle.

4. Doing the "right" thing paves the way for healthier future relationships.

As you move forward in your life, there will be new relationships. Unless you have resolved some of the issues from the failing relationship, they will continue to affect any new relationships. If you are carrying anger and resentment, that is going to be part of who you are and will impact any future relationship.

It's easy to fall into the trap of blaming your ex and finding a new shoulder to cry on and someone to support your victimhood. But that is a poor platform for a new relationship. It will also get old and may well come back to haunt you. There's an old adage that suggests that the very things that attract people initially are also the things that threaten the relationship later. It might feel comforting to have a new love interest support your fight with your ex, but what happens when that fight is resolved or your new partner gets fed up with playing that particular game? Moreover, a new person in your life wants to be part of a new, unique, positive relationship, not someone there to oversee the wreckage of the previous one. New relationships offer the possibility of new beginnings, but to really embrace that idea means leaving old resentments behind.

5. Being "selfish" gives you more clarity.

Not allowing a divorce battle to go on for years also allows you to move on with your life much more quickly. While you are battling with your spouse and his or her attorney in court, that is likely going to dominate your thinking. However, a domestic breakup is a major upheaval, and it is one that provides the opportunity to think through life: the possibilities, your philosophy, and what you want from the future. This is the perfect time for reflection, but that might be difficult if you are still in fight mode, embroiled in a conflict and mired in the dynamics of a failed relationship. The quicker you get to a place of peace, where you can constructively reflect on your life, the sooner you can move forward with greater clarity, focus, and planning.

6. Taking the high ground increases your self-respect.

You can't undo your actions. How you handle anything in your life now, including a separation or a divorce, can't be reversed. Oh sure, you might be able to renegotiate an alimony or child support settlement, but how you act now can never be changed. There are also two important ideas to remember here, too.

Everything you do can always be publicized. In fact, a good rule to live by is to assume that anything you do will go public. If the thought of your behavior going public scares you, then you shouldn't be making the decision or taking that action. How you conduct your-self now will be a basis of how people perceive you later. It's part of your branding.

The second idea is encapsulated in this quote by a Danish philosopher named Kierkegaard:

"Life can only be understood backwards but you have to live it forwards."

The meaning of the events in our lives changes over time. Our perception of events changes, too. One day, you might see your marriage and the separation totally differently from how you do today. In any event, you have to live with how you handle this situation now.

7. An amicable divorce is much better for your children.

I hope that a key consideration in your actions and decisions is the welfare of your children, if you have them. Children need love, stability, trust, and encouragement. Structure is critical, and so the sooner the children can feel safe and secure and free from anxiety, the better. If nothing else, that should be motivation enough for parents to resolve their differences as quickly as possible.

As well as the short-term considerations, there are also the long-term consequences. One goal would be to ensure that your children can have loving relationships with both parents. Whether that is possible will depend on how you and your ex transact your relationship now. So many people alienate their children in one way or another and lose out on being part of their lives during critical periods of development, if not forever. How do you want to be remembered by your children? As a selfish jerk who put their needs way behind yours, or a loving parent who gave them the important things in life?

A good clue as to how you are doing in your children's eyes is how they treat you. Do they want to be with you? Are they eager to rush back home after spending some time with you? When they are with you, are they relaxed and able to have some fun?

If your children are ambivalent about being with you, it is tempting to explain away your children's reticence and caution or even anxiety around you, as a result of your ex's propaganda campaign and attempt to paint you as the bad guy (or gal). There may be some situations where that is indeed the case, but for the most part, people, and children especially, will act more on what they feel about you than what they've been told about you. If you treat your children with love and compassion, they are likely to reciprocate that, regardless of what they have been told. That doesn't mean you should ignore any lies or negativity that have been passed on to your children. Of course, if you and your ex have separated on amicable terms, it's far less likely that there will be much alienation and negativity happening. There won't need to be.

8. Taking this route is beneficial to your ex, too.

In the heat of a marriage meltdown, it is easy to become angry, resentful, and bitter toward your ex. In that state, you may wish all sorts of evil and unpleasant things to befall the person you once loved. However, a more dispassionate look at the situation will reveal that wishing bad things for your ex is not in your best interests for several reasons.

First, if your ex doesn't move on with life, he or she is stuck where they are now, which is fighting with you. In fact, until he or she moves on, you're still on the hook, emotionally if not financially. And the more your ex is stuck in your failed marriage, the less chance you have of moving on yourself. (See the previous section on Your Next Relationship.)

Second, the happier your ex is, the better parent he or she will make for your children. Happier children make for more successful and healthier children. Everyone wins.

Third, when your ex moves on, you are really free to move on, too. So while in the hurt and the anger of a breakup, don't go and shoot yourself in the foot by making life difficult for your ex. It will rebound on to you.

9. A compassionate divorce may fit best with your spiritual beliefs.

If you were married in a church, or in the eyes of God, you might feel some obligation to at least be compassionate and nurturing to each other even when you have decided to break your vows to be together "until death do us part." It may seem as if your marriage is just between you and your spouse, but is it really?

These are the reasons that, for me, justified the "selfish" divorce. They allowed me to take care not just of myself but the entire family.

7 Key Behaviors That Lead To A Selfish Divorce

In Chapter 5, I outlined the behaviors that worked for me in managing my separation and divorce in a positive way. In the last chapter I outlined the reasons why being caring rather than selfish is in your best interests. And in this chapter I will look at seven things you need to do to manage your breakup in a positive fashion.

1. Take responsibility for the past, and *be* responsible moving forward.

There are two important ways in which you need to be responsible. The first is to accept your role in the breakup of your marriage. Most breakups are the result of the couple's collective behavior rather than the fault of any one partner. Yes, there might be some cases where one partner has acted very irresponsibly, but most of the time each partner needs to take at least some responsibility. And to be clear, it's responsibility, *not* fault. In our situation, both Sarah and I changed, and the dynamic of our marriage conspired to make it unrewarding. It was neither Sarah's nor my fault, but we both have to take responsibility for what happened. It is very important to make the distinction between responsibility and fault. Finger-pointing, fault-assigning mode will set you on the path for an adversarial split. Focusing on fault will put you and your brain in a very negative state.

In addition to taking responsibility for your role in the relationship, you need to act responsibly moving forward. That means not just thinking about yourself but about your ex and your children. And it involves the following six traits, too.

2. Be honest.

Being responsible means being trustworthy, and you cannot build trust if you're inconsistent. When you're inconsistent, people will create all manner of conclusions and judgments about your behavior. In short, inconsistency gives others cause to doubt you and to attack you. Honesty is the cornerstone of consistency. If you're honest with yourself and others, there'll be no need to make an effort to be consistent; it will just naturally happen.

Honesty also requires you to be honest with yourself. When you are not playing games, when you are not worried about "positioning" yourself to win a battle, you can afford to be honest. However, as soon as you engage in a fight, honesty disappears. The notion that "truth is the first casualty of war" is present across time and variously attributed to the Greek playwright Aeschylus, the British author Samuel Johnson, and numerous public figures during World War I. Honestly, it's not that important who said it; it's more important you understand that honesty gets sacrificed in a fight.

3. Show appropriate respect to everyone involved.

If you want people to respect you, you have to show respect to them. In this context, respect means recognizing that your ex has the right to his or her opinions even if you disagree with them. Respect means ensuring that your children have what they need to cope with the breakup of the family. Respect means not bad-mouthing your ex, or frankly anyone else. Moreover, respect means putting yourself in your ex's or children's position and acting accordingly. For example, if I was running even a few minutes late to pick up my children, I would text or call to tell them I was on my way. I didn't want them worrying whether I was going to show up. Moreover, if I didn't call there was a chance that my ex would start jumping to conclusions about where I was and what I was doing. The scenarios she might imagine might not have been good. It would at least present an opportunity for her to see me as unreliable and I didn't want that. The imaginations of most people run wild—don't encourage them.

Respect also extends to self-respect. As mentioned in the last chapter, you can't reverse the reality of your reactions. How you manage this situation will be very public and "on the record" forever even if that is just in the memory. And your memory is the one that matters here. Believe me, you will want to look back in the future and be satisfied about how you handled this situation.

4. Love your children by keeping them emotionally safe.

Loving your children means making sure they are safe. It means making sure that they know you love them because you are loving toward them. It means allowing your ex to love them, too. This isn't a competition about who can get the children to love them more. Even in the best and most stable of marriages, each parent brings something unique to the love of their children. Ideally, a mother and father love their children, but that love is manifested in different ways because those parents are individuals with unique gifts, personalities, and ways of loving. In the best, unified marriages, while both parents are consistent in their values and messages toward their children, they manifest that behavior differently.

Loving your children also means taking steps to ensure that they are not put "in the middle" of your disputes with your ex. It also means that you ensure that your children do not feel responsible for your marital situation. In short, loving your children means that they can continue to be children. Needless to say, loving your children means that you ensure their safety and keep them out of dangerous and harmful situations.

Loving you children also means demonstrating to them how to effectively handle conflicts. This is a critical life skill. A breakup may be a crisis, but it is also an opportunity to teach your children how to manage difficulties and setbacks, which might just be the variable most associated with a life of success and achievement. A breakup is tough for everybody but it is also an opportunity to develop resilience.

5. Seek support, not validation.

We are social animals and look to others for validation of our behavior. However, the people you turn to are gong to be your friends who care about you, and they will almost certainly agree with any presentation of your position. I have a therapist friend who says that in this situation, people present a one-sided view to those who are going to support them regardless and then use this dynamic as affirmation that they are right. He says that despite a long career, he's never had any client tell him the following: "I presented both points of view in an objective way to a hundred strangers and 68 percent agreed with me."

A breakup is a time when you need support. That means the people who care about you are there to ensure you take care of yourself. A divorce is not an election or a popularity contest, so don't make it one. Moreover, don't put your friends and even family, many of whom will know your ex, in the impossible position of declaring an opinion one way or another about you or your ex's behavior. They can't possibly know the intricacies of the relationship. They can support you, however, without having to make judgments about your personal situation. It might make you temporarily feel better if all of your friends tell you what an awful person your ex is, but that doesn't mean anything except that things will get meaner.

If you need input about a particular course of action, seek professional help in the form of a qualified counselor who deals with these issues. And a really professional counselor will want to see you and your ex before they can render an opinion. After all, how does the counselor know if what you are saying is an accurate reflection of the situation? Professional guidelines and ethics generally dictate that counselors don't give an opinion until they have seen both parties.

6. Avoid making snap judgments.

Okay, so this is a really hard one even under the best of circumstances. It's hard because the brain needs to structure our experience to make order out of chaos. Any story, even the wrong one, is better than no story at all. The problem with this process is that it is designed to protect us from danger, not to make us right. We make judgments based on very limited information, sometimes just a snippet of gossip, that may be entirely false. We jump to conclusions that are often false, or at best, have a grain of truth in them.

In a domestic breakup, with tensions, anxiety, and bitterness running high, judgments can fly thick and fast. They don't help. When you embrace this non-judgmental approach, you'll find that you are responding and not reacting. And that considered response can usefully include not commenting on other people's views. People are going to believe what they want and you're not going to persuade them out of their positions, which are judgments that serve their own purposes. Let others have their thoughts and opinions. It doesn't matter and there's little value in engaging them. Remember, for the most part, other people's judgments are a reflection of them, not you.

7. Focus on the areas of your life you can control.

Doing the above six behaviors is hard. In the movie *Scent of a Woman*, Al Pacino plays a blind, angry veteran. He visits his brother's house but creates a scene by being typically provocative. As his brother is throwing him out of the house, he asks Al Pacino's character, "Why don't you ever do the right thing?" To which Pacino replies, "I know what the right thing to do is; I just have a hard time doing it." Amen. Doing the right thing is hard and it won't happen by default. You have to work at it. You have to stay focused on it.

Staying focused requires that other areas of your life are in control. If, for example, your business or your health are demanding disproportionate amounts of time and energy, it will be hard, if not impossible, to focus on the behaviors outlined above. Being able to stay consistent, reliable, trustworthy, respectful, and loving toward your children *all* require taking care of yourself. (I'll talk more about how to do this in the next chapter.)

Here's the bottom line: If most aspects of your personal and professional lives are under control, then you will have the energy to stay focused on the key behaviors that will help you make the transition out of your marriage not just manageable, but a positive platform on which to build your future.

CHAPTER EIGHT

The 4 B's:
Core Principles To Help You
Maintain Your Well-Being

The challenges that a domestic breakup bring require you to be on top of your game in every way. If your time, energy, and emotional resources are in high demand in other areas of your life, you just won't be able to focus on acting the way that was established in the last chapter.

This means that you need to take care of yourself. Yes, that's selfish, but "selfish" isn't a dirty word. Selfish gets a bad rap because people confuse it with narcissism, but it's not the same. Narcissism really is selfish—when you put yourself at the center of the universe and everything revolves around you.

For me, taking care of myself in the midst of my divorce focused on four main areas I summarized as the four Bs: Body, Being, Business, and Balance. I developed strategies to help me both focus on and manage these four areas of my life, which kept my coping skills strong.

Here's a closer look at what the Four Bs are and how you can stay healthy in each of these areas:

Body: Maintain physical health through exercise and nutrition.

Exercise is probably the single most important activity that you can do for your health and overall wellness. Apart from the obvious physical benefits, there are huge psychological benefits, too. For example, we now know that the brain can create new brain cells through-out the lifespan. This is especially important in the areas of the brain responsible for memory and learning. Now, it's one thing to create new brain cells; it's anoth-er for them to survive and make a significant difference in how your mind works. Do you know the single big-gest variable that determines whether these brain cells live or die? Physical exercise. In fact, physical exercise is the best stress manager as it helps balance out the neurochemistry of the brain.

What sorts of activities are helpful? Cardio is obviously important for your heart and blood supply. Ensuring a good blood supply is critical for every cell in your body and especially your brain. In fact, people think of car-dio as calorie burning but that's not its main advantage. Sure, you burn calories, but you can do that with other non-cardio exercise. Cardio is good because it main-tains the body and the brain's fuel supply.

Non-cardio activity is also helpful. In fact, the evidence is that you burn fat better with non-aerobic activity than you do with cardio. So walking is a great activity.

Resistance exercises are important. Using weights add to health by developing muscle, which, amongst other things, drives metabolic rate. So lifting weights—not body building—is important for general health, too.

I did all of the above and, in conjunction with my nutri-tion routine (which I will talk about next), I lost twenty pounds of fat and gained fifteen pounds of muscle during my separation.

At the beginning of my separation, my diet wasn't very good, and, of course, as soon as I realized I was going to be single again, I went on the Divorce Diet. But I quickly realized I needed a nutritionist to help me sort out the grains of truth from the nutritional nonsense that is out there.

For me, the biggest benefit of talking to a nutritionist was the understanding I gained about carbs. The Glycemic Index is a way of looking at the real sugar value of carbohydrates. Some foods, probably your favorites, are high-glycemic foods. This means that they have a lot of glucose, and that glucose is quickly absorbed into the bloodstream. Glucose is a very valuable commodity—your body's energy source—and it needs to be conserved. Initially, your blood-glucose level spikes but then it drops as your body removes excess glucose from the blood stream. This stimulates more eating. High-glycemic foods—the so-called white foods, pasta, bread, cookies, baked goods—therefore encourage the storage of glucose as fat and encourage eating.

The issue here is food processing. These so-called "high-glycemic foods" are processed foods. They are processed in the factory, not in your body. As a result, the "free fructose" they contain is rapidly absorbed, leading to the twin problems of fat storage and increased appetite. Natural foods that are not processed in the factory—for example, fruits and vegetables—are broken down in your body. These foods have fructose that is bound to the fiber, and as a result, because fiber passes through the body without being broken down, this fructose is not bio-available and doesn't enter your system. So you can't compare the sugar in a fruit with the sugar in a processed product. Very little of the sugar in the fruit is absorbed, whereas virtually all of the sugar in the processed food is. Once I understood this principle, I was convinced I had to change my diet.

With the help of my nutritionist, I adopted several key methods to help me stay on my plan. I started out measuring and monitoring everything I ate. This gave me a great sense of portion sizes and nutritional value. Then my nutritionist and I worked out my exact schedule of eating for the week: What food, in what quantity, I was going to have at what time, every day. This was very structured, but because it was, it took the guesswork out of the equation. All the food was planned. And I was scheduled to eat something about every three hours.

Of course, I would have to report back to my nutritionist each week on how I had done, and this gave me much-needed accountability. I also devised my own performance metric. I had very specific daily exercise and nutritional goals. I gave myself a half-point each day I met my exercise goals and a half-point for meeting my nutrition goals. In fact, each of the four Bs—

Body, Being, Business, and Balance—had two parts to them, and I gave myself a half-point for each part I achieved each day, for a total of eight half-points, or four points in total. I could thus earn twenty-eight points in a perfect week. This was a very simple but effective metric that allowed me to track my progress through the four core principles.

Being: Nurture your spiritual and emotional well-being.

I was raised in the Church of Latter Day Saints, and prayer and church were an important part of my growing up until my parents divorced. The spiritual side of life has stuck with me and is important to me. I think it is critical for us to put ourselves in context, to constantly be aware that we are a small part of a much larger, interconnected whole. Spirituality is the opposite of selfishness and it gets your thinking oriented outside of you and toward others.

I decided that working on this aspect of my life would consist of two daily activities. One was meditation.

Before I knew anything about meditation, my image of it was of a Tibetan monk in a monastery high up in the Himalayas in classic meditation pose, sitting still and silent for weeks at a time. Obviously, it was difficult to relate to that image. When I eventually learned more about meditation, I discovered that the sense of peace it gave me was amazing. By reducing my brain activity from constant processing to a calm, very relaxed state, I found that I could indeed reach a different state of consciousness.

There are many different types of meditation but the goal of all of them is to get into that mental state between wakefulness and sleep, where consciousness slows down. It's where you stop processing and trying to impose order on your world and just experience it. This helps me enormously by getting myself centered. I felt as if my meditation puts a protective barrier, a space, between "me" and the constant rational processing of life.

This is a very critical point. When I was younger, I buried my emotions and pretended they weren't there. I learned to suck it up and carry on. On one level this gave me some skill in not allowing my emotions to control me, at least not overtly. But of course, subconsciously, these emotions were still very much in play and affecting my life.

Learning how to meditate helped take my emotional control to a completely different level. Now, instead of burying my feelings, I could view them dispassionately. Meditation allowed me to see my emotions as passing states, as objects with which I didn't need to engage. This really allowed me to be freed of emotional conflict, and I think was a big reason why I was able to not get caught up in the drama that usually accompanies a separation.

The other commitment I made was to read from some sort of "spiritual" book every day. These books weren't necessarily religious books, but they were books that had a spiritual dimension. Books that fell into this category were:

- The Way of the Superior Man by David Deida

- Loving What Is by Byron Katie

- *The Dhammapada* by Eknath Easwaran

- The Four Agreements by Don Miguel Ruiz

- ...and several others on Christ and Christianity

I also developed a different way of reading these books. I would read until I reached an "aha" moment. When I came across a concept that was both novel and profound for me, I stopped reading. I wrote down the concept, thought about it, and pondered it for the remainder of the day. This way I really considered the idea, what it was, and how it was relevant for me. This made reading much more meaningful to me. My reading wasn't determined by time or the chapter, but by the importance of the ideas that I encountered.

I learned a lot. Some days I would read for thirty minutes, some days for five. The time wasn't important; the ideas were. I gave myself a half-point every day when I meditated and another half-point when I read and focused on a spiritual idea. When I read a spiritual book, my one goal was to open my horizon, to open my mind to new possibilities. When you are closed off to new ideas, it's very easy to get stuck in a rut.

Business: Continue to grow professionally.

Whether one likes it or not, one's job and the business of making money take up a lot of time and energy. And as I pointed out in the previous chapter, if you're experiencing problems at work, your ability to focus on conducting a "selfish" divorce will be impaired. So, focusing on one's business is important.

Here, I did exactly what I did above for the spiritual domain. I read and I considered. In this case I made it a point to read parts of a business book every day. Just as with the spiritual book mentioned above, I would read until I reached an "aha" moment. Again, when I came across a valuable idea, I stopped reading. I wrote down the idea and then considered how that concept could be implemented in my own business.

The second part of this plan was, where practical, to actually implement the idea or some variant of it. An example to this would be learning the skill of creating long- and short-term business goals. Now, it's easy to say you want to make a lot of money but it's another thing altogether to write and execute a plan to create a successful business. Currently, my favorite topic is on direct marketing and books such as *80/20* by Perry Marshall, *The Art of the Sale* by Philip Delves Broughton, and the classic *Think and Grow Rich* by Napoleon Hill.

Again I gave myself a half-point each day for both reading a business book and for implementing the ideas I had uncovered.

Balance: Invest in growing and maintaining meaningful relationships.

When I think of balance in my life, I don't think that means I have to spend equal amounts of time in the different silos of my life. Instead, I define balance as ensuring that you manage the relationships in your life and give them the love and attention they need. So for me, balance isn't about time; it's about quality of relationships. It means that I need to focus on those meaningful relationships, investing some time and being thoughtful about them.

One way I stay focused on my relationships and maintain the balance in my life is by asking the question: If I were to die in a year, what would I want to have achieved in my relationships? What would I not want to leave undone?

For example, with my children I would want to teach them about love. I would want to invest in my relationship with them by showing I loved them. And in doing so, I want to show them how to love. Another lesson I want to teach my kids is impulse control and the ability to delay gratification, as I mentioned earlier in reference to the Stanford Marshmallow Study.

So for me, balance is investing in my important relationships. In the context of the four core principles, I would focus on two relationships each week for extra-special attention. I would do something special for those two people. That might mean sending flowers or a note, reaching out to a friend, shooting fun videos, anything that would deepen or preserve our connection.

For instance, assume you wanted to start fixing your relationship with your ex. I don't mean that you're trying to get back together but that you want to move on and you want him or her to move on. You might say, "I want to show that I am reliable and trustworthy, and to prove it I will call my children each night at 8:00 p.m." Now, this does two things. First, it's a way to show your children that you still love them and are committed to them. Second, your ex will be watching and making sure you are consistent, and when you are, this will go a long way in proving you will step up and will be there for your family.

When I put that thought, time, and effort in a relationship each week, I would give myself a half-point, or one full point if I did it for two people as I had planned.

Attending to these four core principles really helped give me energy, self-confidence, and above all a sense that I was living life the way I think it should be lived. This gave me a sense of contentment, which in turn, allowed me to manage my breakup in the way that I wanted.

Take Care of Yourself with the Four Core Principles: A Checklist

If you decide to incorporate any or all of the four Bs into your life as you navigate separation and divorce, you may find the following checklist helpful:

1. Body

- Devise a regular workout schedule that includes cardio, anaerobic activity, and some resistance exercises.

- Take control of your nutrition by eating clean, eliminating processed foods, and minimizing "free fructose" in sodas and other sugary products.

2. Being

- Meditate every day, even if just for a few minutes.

- Read a spiritual book and take one lesson from it to consider each day.

3. Business

- Read a business book and take one lesson from it.

- Consider that lesson and try to incorporate it into your life.

4. Balance

- Choose two relationships and give them proper attention and love. Invest in those you love.

If you do all of these activities on a daily basis, you can score four points a day. A great week is a twenty-eight!

CHAPTER NINE

Are You ABLE To Conduct A "Selfish" Divorce?

I have outlined why a "selfish" approach to a breakup can work to the benefit of both parties. Taking care of each other's needs means a less stressful separation and includes benefits for both parties, most notably, the ability to move on. I have outlined what that requires and the steps you can take to ensure you're in the best shape to manage this effectively.

Nonetheless, you might still be having great difficulty embracing the "selfish divorce" philosophy and/or knowing how to implement it. In this chapter, I will tell you what you need to do to get out of your rut and quickly on to a more fulfilling life.

There are three broad types of people who have difficulty following the selfish divorce approach. Each type faces specific challenges in moving from the unhelpful position they currently occupy to a more productive one.

First are the **Egotists.** These people are the ones who have to win. Their divorce is a game, and they are not prepared to lose. For them, it's about getting one over on their ex, no matter how much it costs or how long it takes. They are fueled by anger and resentment and can't see beyond their negative feelings.

Next are the **Drop-outs.** In some ways, they are the opposite of the Egotists in that they don't want to fight. Passivity is their way of fighting. They are the passive part of passive-aggressive. They opt out of meaningful discussion and avoid the issues.

Finally, there are the **Resenters.** These folks do negotiate and rationally accept the need for equitable settlements but they bear grudges. They accept the need to settle equitably but resent and detach.

These categories can sometimes reflect the overall personalities of the people involved; in other cases, they may just represent how an individual reacts to the specific situation of going through a divorce. For example, people with a narcissistic personality disorder or borderline personality disorder are probably going to be over-represented amongst the egotists. Typically, these personality disorders don't take responsibility for their own actions and attack everyone else as a form of defense. But not *all* "divorce egotists" suffer from personality disorders—some simply react in a truly selfish, aggressive manner.

Regardless of which category you may fall into, to achieve control of your emotions and impulses, you'll need to focus on four things that collectively spell out the acronym ABLE.

"A" Is for Attention

The things you spend time focusing on will determine your attitude, emotions, and even brain state. Think of attention as a lens through which everything is filtered. It will determine your perceptions. There's a concept in neuroscience called "top-down processing." That is when we have a perception and we impose that perception on what we see. For example, you may have seen the image that can be viewed as either the profile of a young girl or the face of an old woman. At first, you don't see anything as you attempt bottom-up processing. Bottom-up processing involves having no perception and letting the image create your perception. But once you see the young girl and/or the old woman, you can't look at the image without seeing them. That's top-down processing—you have a perception that you impose or force onto what you see.

A lot of time we use top-down processing. We are fixed in our perceptions and we see what we want to see, often to the exclusion of alternative perceptions. So where we focus, where we put our attention, is critical. For example, if you spend all your time focusing on your ex's behavior and faults, you aren't looking at yours, or even seeing them. You're also painting your ex as the "villain" and ignoring the fact that you, too, are partially responsible for creating the current situation.

If you attend to the principles outlined in this book, that positive focus will create the right mindset for an adaptive approach to your breakup.

"B" Is for Behavior

As you navigate your divorce, people are going to make all sorts of judgments about you, and most of them will be based on your behavior. (Some perceptions will be based on gossip but there's not a lot you can do about that.) That's important, because how other people see you (and how you see yourself) can cement you into your role as an egotist, a drop-out, or a resenter—or free you from those roles so that you can pursue a "selfish divorce."

Be aware that what you do now determines what you do next and which role you'll fall into. For example, if you have hired the most aggressive attorney in town and announced that you are determined to nail your ex, all subsequent perceptions of you will be based on the idea that you intend to show no mercy. (In other words, you'll have confirmed that you're an egotist.) So now, you have a choice: Do you confirm others' opinions by taking your ex for all he or she is worth, or do you choose a different, more compassionate behavior?

It takes a lot of wisdom and courage to change course, but adjusting your behavior is often crucial to conducting a civil, mutually beneficial divorce. Remember, while the consequences of your actions might be reversible (e.g., a change in terms of an agreement), the memory and record of your behavior is irreversible.

"L" Is for Language

Words are important. The language you use has emotional connotations. Words lead to thoughts and thoughts to emotions. I mentioned earlier in the book that during our marriage Sarah and I didn't continually throw the "divorce" word around, or really use it at all. "Divorce" is a loaded word with many emotional connotations. The more this word is used, the more of a reality it becomes.

In fact, there is some interesting new neuroscience research that suggests that words set up *images* of the action the words describe, in this case images of getting a divorce. Words also stimulate the neurological activity associated with actually doing that action. For example, if someone says to a friend, "He kicked the ball," the friend will not only imagine the kicking action; the motor areas of his brain involved in actual kicking are activated—even though he doesn't produce the gross motor movement of kicking. What's even more interesting, if the speaker uses "kicking" in a metaphor (i.e., "He kicked the bucket"), the same motor areas in the listener are activated!

Here's my point: Talking about divorce stimulates images of divorce-related activities and makes a divorce more likely. And once a divorce has been initiated, using words that convey anger, resentment, blame, and victim-thinking encourage a negative tone in your interactions and motivations. Conversely, though, using language that evokes teamwork, respect, and well-being will have the opposite effect—and may very well make the difference in experiencing a "nice" divorce as opposed to a nasty one.

So, wherever possible, use positive words or at least not emotionally loaded ones. "Resolution" is better than "resentment."

Also, remember that the language you use when speaking to yourself is just as impactful as the language you use when speaking to others. The conversations you have in your head are going to shape to the conversations you have with other people.

"E" Is for Emotion

Emotions are valuable signals that are meant to get our attention. For example, anger is an indicator of the perception that you're being treated unfairly. Frustration is an indicator of the perception that you're being thwarted in your achievement of some objective. Guilt is an indicator of the perception that you have violated some moral code. Each emotion is tied to a perception. Ideally, we learn to manage those emotions and use them to address the underlying situations that are causing them.

One of the key words here is "perception." You may perceive that you have been treated unfairly but it's possible that your definition of "fair" is unreasonable. To use a rather extreme example, you might be so entitled that any time someone doesn't do what you want, you might think of that as gross unfairness, which stimulates anger.

Because emotions are based on perceptions, and because perceptions can be distorted, the best first response to an emotion is to conduct a reality check.

Let's suppose you can't reach your ex at a time mutually agreed upon for a phone call. You might think, She's probably gone out after work drinking with some of her colleagues. Typical! Totally irresponsible! She's blowing me off. How disrespectful! Okay, I'll show her!

However, the reality may be that your ex is on the side of the road with a flat tire or tending to one of your sick children. Humans have the power to create a perception of what is happening and then believe it based on zero evidence whatsoever. The perception leads to an emotion, which then feeds off itself and builds and builds, especially in a potentially tense and fraught situation like a breakup.

You have to go out of your way to manage these tendencies if you want to enjoy the advantages of the selfish divorce. That's why consideration, empathy, and thoughtfulness are important. They minimize the sort of negative projection that can cause so many problems.

There are times when anger and frustration are legitimate. However, it doesn't do you any good to stay stuck in the emotion. That's where exercise, meditation in its broadest sense, and a spiritual connection—part of the four core principles described in the last chapter—come into play. They all help you move beyond the emotion and put it in perspective.

Listen to your emotions but don't be led by them. You can observe them but you don't have to believe them or indulge them.

So how do these considerations affect egotists, dropouts, and resenters specifically? In the remainder of this chapter, I'll take a closer look—and I'll also point out which of the four core principles (Body, Being, Business, and Balance) each category should focus on.

Becoming More ABLE If You're an Egotist

The egotist really has to be careful what he or she wishes. There are plenty of examples of people winning the divorce battle but losing the war. I personally know two examples of people who were determined to win at all costs, and in both cases that macho attitude came back to haunt them.

In the first case, a guy spent a fortune getting custody of his children from a common-law wife. But anyone who knew this guy knew he wasn't exactly a stay-at-home dad. Three months after he "won" a messy and very expensive legal contest, he arranged to pay for his ex-partner to look after the kids as he decided to take off and jet around the world with his new girlfriend.

In the second case, an older man fought a fierce custody campaign that cost well into six figures. One of the issues he had was some serious agitation with his teenage son. The father prevailed and took custody of his son and daughter and brought them into his home with his new fiancée. However, the tension between the man and the boy got so bad the fiancée decided to call off the wedding.

Dale Carnegie said, "Nobody wins an argument." There's always a price for winning, and when you have to deal with your opponent over the long-term, as you do if you share children, you need to be careful about how you are setting up the future.

- **Attention: Focus on the future.** Your attention needs to be turned not to the grievances you feel about the past but on the possibilities for your future. Think about the positive goals you want to achieve and the life you want to lead. Take attention off the frustration and anger of the present and look to the life ahead. Stop looking at all of your ex's faults and acknowledge your own responsibility.

- **Behavior: Find control by being calm.** Don't act like a macho ass or a psycho bitch. You might think it's cool, but honestly, it looks dumb and it will get you into trouble. Sure, your friends will encourage you and cheer you on, but they won't be there to pick up the pieces.

Remember, someone who is in control rarely has to shout and name-call. The person who has it together doesn't have to jump up and down, threaten, and accuse. Negotiating from a position of dignity and respect will almost always be much better in the long run. Again, you can win a battle but lose the war. And remember that if the other party is really trying to goad you on, the best response is to not get sucked in. Allowing somebody to pull your strings only encourages them even more.

Sure, it's easy to find fault with anybody. But how about looking at your ex's strengths, too?

- **Language: Back away from blame.** The egotist uses the language of abuse, threat, and blame. All this does is make a fight inevitable and keeps the egotist in fight mode. The language needs to change to reflect an attempt to resolve the situation without fighting and to recognize the egotist's role in the situation.

Keywords to remember: responsibility, amicable

- **Emotion: Work to defuse anger.** The emotion for the fighter is high levels of stress and anger. The egotist needs to calm down. Egotists may think that they have it under control but the fact is that the continued high levels of brain arousal that are associated with these mood states will take a toll on energy and health.

I understand there will be times of anger and frustration, but the key is not to let those two emotions hijack your best efforts to build a better life.

- The Four Core Principles: If you're an egotist, you would do well to emphasize two of the core principles. First, focus on Being, because spiritual understanding and recognition of the forces outside of yourself will give you a healthier perspective. Second, focus on Body, since physical exercise should help reduce some of the stress you're feeling and will also aid in achieving better mental balance.

Becoming More ABLE If You're a Drop-out

The drop-out is characterized by a passivity and unwillingness to engage. Although this can be less damaging than an egotistical fight, it still has its own set of problems.

- **Attention: Push yourself to participate.** The drop-out's focus is on not engaging and absenteeism. If you're a drop-out, you need to put aside the resentment and the fear and participate. Participation requires putting your attention on the important things you're currently facing: the future and welfare of your children, your ex, and yourself.

- **Behavior: Build bridges with baby steps.** Being passive doesn't build bridges or a platform for the future. The lack of contact can be hurtful and leaves way too much open to interpretation. It might seem like disengagement is an acceptable strategy because it seems better than fighting, but there are better alternatives.

Drop-outs often are very afraid that for one reason or another they can't engage in meaningful discussion. This could be because of their ex's inability to create an environment for such a discussion or their own inability to communicate effectively. In this case, start with small steps. Begin by addressing one small, less loaded issue. For many drop-outs the key is the ability of both sides to create an effective communication environment.

- **Language: Use your words.** Drop-outs don't talk much, so while they don't inflame the situation with words, they *can* inflame it with silence. They also miss the opportunity to create new ways of relating and building new relationships moving forward.

Keywords to remember: communicate, engagement

- **Emotion: Manage your anxiety.** The prevailing emotions for drop-outs are resentment, frustration, and (mostly) fear about what will happen if the drop-out tries to reach out. That fear of communication needs to be overcome. If necessary, help and support from others can help break the ice and reduce the anxiety. A friend or even a counselor can guide you on how, when, and where to initiate contact and manage it effectively.

- **The Four Core Principles:** As a drop-out, you should emphasize Balance, as that will keep you focused on the real importance of relationships and the need to make extra effort to recognize the important people in your life.

Becoming More ABLE If You're a Resenter

Resenters are characterized by a rational acceptance of the need for an equitable settlement but an inability to emotionally embrace it.

- **Attention: Stop looking in the rearview mirror.** The resenter's focus needs to move off everything he or she is losing and on to what can be gained moving forward. It's almost as if the resenter is stuck looking at life in the rearview mirror. The fact is that the relationship didn't work out and that arrangements need to be made for the future (preferably, in a way that allows all parties to move on). So accept reality. Look forward! Remember, resurrection, not resentment!

- **Behavior: Don't be a sore loser.** The resenter at least has the good grace to try to do the right thing by engaging in sensible settlement discussions. There's an adage that what people take away most from any interaction is how you made them feel. If you reached an agreement about the tangibles of moving forward, it doesn't cost extra to be accepting of the situation rather than resentful. And it will significantly improve the outcome for everybody, but especially yourself, if you can act with grace and dignity rather than seeming like a poor loser.

- **Language: Get rid of "what if," "if only," and "poor me."** Acceptance and agreement need to replace resentment for the person in this category. Gratitude is better than grumpiness. The conversations you have with yourself and others need to reflect acceptance and a willingness to move forward.

Keywords to remember: acceptance, agreement

- **Emotion: Focus on forgiveness.** "Resentment is like taking poison and expecting the other person to die." This adage is entirely accurate. The re- senter is the one who will suffer the most from holding onto bitterness. It's not adaptive and will hold them back significantly. It's time for resent- ers to put their bitterness behind them for their own good—and focusing on forgiveness (of your ex, yourself, and any other parties involved) is the most effective way to make that happen.

- **The Four Core Principles:** If you're a resenter, focus on Being, since spiritual exposure might help you see the bigger picture and allow you to focus on your blessings rather than resenting what you see as injustices.

CHAPTER TEN

Building A Positive Future —
Even If Your Ex Isn't On Board

In the movie *War Horse* there is a wonderfully insightful line about love and relationships. After a husband does something incredibly impulsive that threatens his and his wife's security, he implores his wife not to hate him for his actions.

"I might hate you more but that doesn't mean I love you less," she replies.

In this scene, Richard Curtis and Lee Hall have nailed something very important about relationships with all the succinctness of outstanding professional screenwriters: You can love and "hate" the same person. You can love some things they do and detest others. In an intimate relationship you know each other so well that there are bound to be things that aggravate you about your partner. Of course, in the beginning, when you really don't know someone at all, it's easy to build your perception of them around an overly positive image of a person who can hang the moon.

Natural Negativity

The mind likes simplicity. It is confusing to feel love and hate, even though we can clearly feel both toward the same person. So, in the romantic infatuation phase of a relationship, our perceptions are ridiculously positive...and it feels great. During a breakup there's the reverse tendency to make perceptions ridiculously negative...and it sucks. These extremes serve the purpose of avoiding the reality of mixed emotions. As Judith Viorst said in her book *Necessary Losses,* "You can love or hate your partner with equal force."

The point is, in the deconstruction of your relationship it's almost a natural tendency to emphasize the negative. The selfish divorce model is designed to prevent you from falling into that trap. The tools in this book and the principles on which they are based are intended to help you recognize that your partner and the relationship don't need to be trashed or reconstructed through a negative lens. Both have evolved into something different than they once were, but that doesn't make your ex or your marriage terrible or a disaster.

So, hopefully, you have embraced the benefits of the selfish divorce and have made a commitment to adapt your lifestyle to the four core principles, which will give you the energy and resources to move forward with your life. Of course, nothing is easy, and you might encounter some obstacles along the way.

One obstacle could be that while you are ready to embrace the approach outlined in this book, your soon-to-be ex isn't. He or she might still want to fight, avoid the issues, or not communicate with you. Here are some tips to manage typical situations where your former partner doesn't want to participate.

1. Don't get sucked into negativity and bitterness. As mentioned at the beginning of this chapter, breakups tend to be the perfect setting for hostility and negativity to take root. Therefore, there's a chance that you are now facing an ex who is angry and resentful.

While the natural response when you're being attacked or even abused is to fight back, the fact is that in this situation, especially if you are already living separately, you really can turn the other cheek. If your ex is determined to be angry and bitter, there's not a lot you can do about that, but you don't have to follow suit. Some people thrive on conflict and drama and by not engaging you're taking away one of their biggest weapons. Again, this isn't just about taking the moral high ground; it's adaptive. Keeping out of the angry, bitter mindset is good for your health and your future.

When faced with an angry attack, recognize that winning is not letting the attack get to you and winding you up. **Take ten deep breaths and switch your focus quickly onto something else. Some physical activity helps.** It may help to remember Oscar Wilde's words: "Forgive your enemies—they'll hate you for it."

2. "No comment" is appropriate. Just because you're asked a question, you don't have to reply. Again, some people can be very manipulative and are good at putting others in a bind. Such people will try to make you feel guilty or responsible, but at the very least, buy some time to consider your response. You don't need to engage if you feel you're being put on the spot. Having a stock reply ready like, "I need to think about that," or, "I'm not ready to discuss that right now," can help prevent being pressured into a conversation you don't want to have.

Decide on a simple response that you can use when you're put on the spot. It needs to be automatic so that you don't hesitate and get pushed into a conversation you don't want to have.

3. Establish appropriate boundaries. One of the most difficult aspects of a breakup is the change in expectations of each other and the creation of new boundaries. The boundaries that you have as a divorced couple are quite different from those that you had when married. Exactly what those new boundaries are can be difficult to negotiate. It's important, therefore, to be able to communicate and agree about this. If the arrangements are that you pick up the kids at 5:00 p.m., pick them up at that time. Remember, being consistent, reliable, and trustworthy reinforces good boundaries.

While this may sound straightforward, there can be grey areas. Sure, your agreement stipulates where and when you pick up your children. But what if your ex has a car accident and needs help? Is he or she going to call you? How will you respond? What if the washing machine breaks down? Or one of your children is home from school sick?

You have to determine the boundaries that work for you. As a rule of thumb, however, the parent who has the responsibility for the children at the time of any event is the one who has to deal with whatever situation arises without involving the other parent—unless it's a very serious situation. One thing you have to be clear about: You do not respond out of guilt, obligation, or habit.

It's not possible to legislate for every situation, so consider your actions carefully. As a general rule, if it doesn't feel right, it probably isn't.

4. Create the right communication environment. If you want anyone to talk to you openly, you must create the right communication environment. This means listening to what the other person has to say without judgment or criticism. You might not agree with what your ex is saying but you do need to respect him or her. People will talk openly to you when they feel safe; otherwise they won't—and you might miss out on important information.

Listening is hard for a lot of people, especially in an emotionally charged situation. As the other person is talking, it is easy to start thinking of your rebuttals and focusing on the conversation in your head rather than the one supposedly going on in front of you. When this happens, both people can walk away from the same conversation with very different opinions of what was discussed and decided. As George Bernard Shaw says, "The problem with communication is the illusion that it has taken place." Fortunately, there's a solution: actively listening. Listening can tell you a lot about the person speaking, so it's good to pay attention.

It may help to remember that listening to someone isn't agreeing with them, and neither is respecting their right to a viewpoint. It's okay to acknowledge an understanding of what the person is saying. Doing so doesn't mean you agree or that you intend to tolerate hurtful behavior.

It *does* enable you to move forward without misunderstandings.

5. Reinforce the positive. People learn best by trial and success. Trial and error tells you what NOT to do; trial and success tells you what to do. The best way to change your or someone else's behavior is to reinforce positive actions. No matter how small that action may be, if it's positive, it needs to be acknowledged.

So when your ex is ranting at you, you do not respond. If, when he or she has finished, they sort of apologize or recognize that the rant went too far, you acknowledge that in an appreciative way. For instance, you can say: "I know it can be frustrating," "I appreciate your recognizing that was a bit harsh," or some other response that validates their relatively positive behavior. And when you are reinforcing positive behavior, don't just say it; mean it. Otherwise you'll sound patronizing and that will have completely the opposite effect.

6. Look at the good. It is easy in the wake of a breakup to focus on the "failure" of the relationship and the "fault" of each party, but this isn't helpful or adaptive. After stress or trauma of any type, there are two choices, and which choice you make has major implications for your life. A negative focus will keep you locked in a depressive state with serious repercussions for you. The brain will stay in that emotional state unless you make a specific effort to change it. There's a lot of evidence that the resilience that can be developed in the wake of a trauma or a loss is beneficial for overall health and brain vitality, long after the trauma has ended. Life is hard, so don't compound it by falling into negativity and victimhood. Seriously, you are training your brain and your emotions, and this is a huge transition point.

Focus on the positive aspects of the situation. It's a chance to review and reconstruct your life. Sure, they'll be challenges, but honestly, that's the only way you will grow and develop into the person you want to be. Yes, it's going to be work and effort, but personally, I have never had anything that was really valuable just happen to drop in my lap. This new beginning will force you to change, and the reality is that most of us need to be forced to make real change in our lives.

7. Be the best version of you. Breakups don't normally happen when things are going great. This relationship didn't work for all sorts of reasons. You now have the opportunity to really focus on being the best version of you.

The best version of ourselves manifests when we can look at our reflections in the mirror and feel good about the way we are conducting our lives. The four core principles will help you find meaning and purpose as they also train you to take care of yourself mentally and physically. The best version of you doesn't start when you begin another relationship, or in a few months, or when you get a new job. The best version of you starts now.

Putting It All Together: My Current Life Chapter

It's been three years since Sarah and I divorced. The approach we adopted at the time of our breakup has meant that each of us could move forward in our lives without resentment and bitterness. We have developed great boundaries that allow us to communicate freely without putting any unreasonable demands on each other. The relationship that I have with Sarah and her husband, Trevor, has allowed us to remain cordial and friendly, which has been a huge plus for our children.

I know my children have benefitted. Unlike me, they didn't have to listen to their mother talking about their father. Neither of them were taken on hour-long car rides where they had to listen to their parents' problems. Neither of them feel they have to take care of anyone but themselves. They are completely free to love both their mother and their father—and their stepfather. They are comfortable when we are alone and when we are all together. They know it wasn't their divorce.

There are times, specifically at holidays, when we all hang out together. For example, I will join Trevor and Sarah and our children at Easter. On Christmas we make sure we are all together for some part of Christmas Day. The children really love this, and it feels natural to them. If I happen to be traveling and find myself in the same city as Sarah and Trevor, we would probably arrange to have dinner together. This not only helps our children; it helps us. It enables us to see that our divorce was not a train wreck that ruined our lives but a part of life that we have put in a proper and adaptive perspective.

A divorce is hard because nobody likes change, especially the many life changes that come with a breakup. However, if you handle the process with dignity and respect, you can move forward without hurting others and, more specifically, yourself. Then you'll be best prepared for the next chapter in your life.

Made in the USA
San Bernardino, CA
15 December 2014